✠

This book belongs to _____

Confirmed on _____

At _____

Signature of parish priest _____

Signature of Bishop _____

# Faith Confirmed

**Peter Jackson** read theology at Oxford, where he also qualified as a teacher and prepared for ordination. He served in two parishes, in Oxford and Malvern, before becoming Chaplain of Aldenham School. In 1990 he was appointed Chaplain and Head of Religious Studies at Harrow School. He is now Assistant Rector and Director of Education at St Patrick's Episcopalian Parish, Washington DC.

He has written textbooks for use in schools and was involved in the production of the SCAA model syllabuses. He has also lectured in the Department of Education at King's College, London and broadcast on Radio 4 and local radio.

**Chris Wright** has taught extensively both in Britain and abroad. He has been a lecturer in Religious Education at King's College, London and Director of the Anglican International School in Jerusalem. He has published a number of books on the teaching of Christianity to teenagers and young adults, including *Key Christian Beliefs, Life Issues* and *Jesus for Today*. He is now Headteacher of St Peter's High School and International Language College, Stoke-on-Trent.

Other books by Peter Jackson

*The Ways of God* (Herga Press, 1991)

*The People of God* (Herga Press, 1996)

*The Church of God* (Herga Press, 1996)


Other books by Chris Wright

*Key Christian Beliefs* (Lion Publishing, 1995)

*Jesus for Today* (Oxford University Press, 1996)

*Life Issues* (Lion Publishing, 1997)

# *Faith Confirmed*

PETER JACKSON AND CHRIS WRIGHT

First published in Great Britain 1999

Society for Promoting Christian Knowledge
36 Causton Street
London SW1P 4ST
www.spckpublishing.co.uk

The authors and the publisher would like to express their gratitude to Jeffrey John
and Bishop David Stancliffe, and others at Affirming Catholicism,
for their help in bringing this project to fruition.

*British Library Cataloguing-in-Publication Data*
A catalogue record for this book is available from the British Library.

ISBN 978–0–281–05129–8

7  9  10  8

Typeset by David Benham, Norwich, Norfolk
First printed in Great Britain by the Bath Press Ltd, Blantyre, Glasgow
Reprinted in China by New Era Printing Company

# CONTENTS

# CONTENTS

# WHAT THIS BOOK IS FOR

In the introduction to this book we compare confirming our faith in Jesus to deciding to travel with a really accurate map through life. Each chapter forms part of the map. When you look at a map, you have to find your bearings; similarly, it's best to glance through the layout of each chapter before you read it properly.

Each chapter begins with a story or stories and pictures, which are designed to provide a bridge between ideas and experiences which are already familiar to you and the Christian beliefs which you will need to find out about. More factual information is provided in green boxes headed 'Christian beliefs'. You can use these for reference or to explore the ideas in greater detail. There are further stories and explanations later in the chapter to deepen your understanding.

Each chapter concludes with three standard sections:

**Thinking it through** provides you with some questions to ask yourself. They can also be used to open up group discussion. To answer them, you can turn back and look through the chapter but you can also draw on your own experience.

**Bible Study** can be used by you on your own or in a group. It should help you to understand how Christian beliefs are rooted in the Bible.

**For prayer and reflection** provides you with a prayer which you may use privately or say together in a group. You may also like to make up your own prayers reflecting what you have learned from the chapter. The great thing about making up prayers is that it involves your feelings as well as your mind. In prayer, the whole of your personality can be engaged.

## To those leading groups preparing for confirmation

We have aimed in writing this book to make a simple, accessible and attractive presentation of what Anglicans believe. Inevitably, individuals may quibble over details and points of emphasis but we believe that a coherent exposition of Anglican belief is possible and desirable if we are effectively to draw people into active, thoughtful and committed membership of the Church.

The main practical principle behind the writing of this book is that people need bridges between their own experience and Christian concepts. These are best provided by pictures and stories. Once contact has been made between the reader and the main Christian concept, the group leader can then choose from a wide variety of material.

Each chapter is laid out in much the same way, in sections, as described above. The time available

*Confirmation classes introduce us to the Christian 'map' for our journey through life.*

and the age and ability of your group will all affect how much coverage you can allocate to each section.

The book has been designed very much to be the personal possession of each reader. It will be used particularly by those preparing for confirmation but it will also be valuable to those who have already gone some way on their personal Christian journey and wish simply to know more about the Christian faith. We hope that readers will read some or all of the book on their own.

Finally, our own experience has led us to believe that the 'For prayer and reflection' section can be particularly rewarding. It is often when a group or individuals come to compose their own prayers that they are able to give personal expression to the Christian beliefs they have studied. Then their hearts as well as their minds become engaged.

# *I*NTRODUCTION

When we confirm something we say yes. At confirmation we say yes to Jesus' call to follow him on our journey through life. We confirm our faith in him. Parents and godparents will usually have said yes for us when we were babies and unable to speak for ourselves at baptism, but confirmation gives *us* the chance to say yes.

We have all had the experience of getting lost. This can happen because we have either no map or an inadequate one. Confirming our faith in Jesus is like deciding to travel with a really accurate map through life. This book aims to help you become familiar with the main features of the 'Christian map'.

On the contents page you will find its landmarks. Some of these will be familiar to you and others new. Although it will make sense if you read the book on your own, we hope that you share it with others. Just as planning a journey is more fun when you discuss it with others, so Christianity makes more sense when it's experienced and lived with other people. We hope also that you will refer back to this guide after your confirmation. On long journeys, we have to keep on checking our directions. To carry the 'journey' picture a bit further: why not see confirmation as a time to take stock of where you have come from and seek God's help in preparing for what lies ahead?

*The Bible and Christian tradition provide a 'compass' for Christians.*

*'The heavens are telling the glory of God' (Psalm 19.1) How does this scene from nature make you feel? Have you ever felt a sense of awe and wonder at creation? Which natural scenes take your breath away?*

# *G* OD

*'Do you believe and trust in God the Father?'*

**'I believe in God, the Father almighty, creator of heaven and earth.'**

If you are reading this book you believe in God. But where did this belief come from? Maybe you were brought up to believe in God by your parents, or saw God at work in people you respected and looked up to. Maybe you began to believe in God from reading the Bible. Maybe you started to believe in a Creator God as you looked around at the beautiful design in the world. Or maybe you started to feel that there was an unseen hand guiding your life, that coincidences were signs of God, present through the circumstances and the people you met.

Some people, like David's parents, started to believe in God as a result of a crisis. David had been playing with an air rifle and got into trouble with the police. He became more upset than anyone could guess and out of desperation killed himself. His parents were devastated. Their world had come to an end. All their hopes had been destroyed. Their life became one long nightmare as they were confronted with newspaper reporters and police interviews. However, in their despair both of his parents turned to God. Their son's death became a religious experience for them – they woke up to what was important in life, turned to God, began reading the Bible and going to church and within a year became confirmed in the Church.

# How do we know God?

God is waiting to enter into a loving relationship with each of us. He reveals himself in a number of ways.

## Through the Bible and the Church

The Bible is our main source for understanding how God has acted and how Jesus came into the world to save us.

As we will see in Chapter 8, the Bible was produced over a very long period. Therefore, it provides us with a unique record of how countless generations experienced God's presence and actions and bore witness to them.

Christians believe that God inspired the different authors of the books of the Bible to write them so that his revelation of himself should be kept alive for later generations.

The Church has done this by translating and copying the Bible but also by teaching about the Bible and applying it afresh to new circumstances. It is a living book kept alive by the living community of the Church.

That is one of the reasons why we have provided suggestions for Bible study in this book. We cannot hear the Bible as the living Word of God unless we study it and give it time to speak to us.

## Through his creation

Have you ever felt a sense of awe and wonder at nature – maybe standing under a waterfall, or on top of a mountain or being caught in a thunderstorm? Many people have felt God's powerful presence in the world he created. Its beauty and majesty have revealed God's beauty and majesty to them.

*What words come to mind when you look at this window? The designer was trying to capture in glass some of God's qualities. What qualities do you think he has managed to describe?*

## Through experiences in life

What does it mean to say a person has a conscience? Have you ever felt your conscience telling you to do something or to stop doing something? Where does your sense of right and wrong come from?

Christians believe that God speaks to people through their conscience. They can develop their conscience by learning about what the Bible and the Church's tradition teach.

Sometimes we have experiences which make us stand back and ask 'where did that come from?' God speaks to us through our everyday life – through the people we meet and the things that happen. Sometimes people dismiss these experiences as coincidences and ignore the fact that God may be speaking to us through them.

Sometimes God speaks to people in an unmistakable way. Such people say that they have experienced a conversion in which their lives have been shaken up and turned around. However, for other people their conversion is very gradual and may take many years – it is a slow realization that their values and attitudes are changing and being brought more in line with God's wishes for them.

## Through prayer

God is a personal God. We believe that God speaks to us through prayer. As with any relationship we need to spend time together – to talk and listen to each other. This is what prayer is – a time of talking and listening to God. Without prayer the relationship would become dry. Prayer is the way we communicate with God.

*What is going on in this photograph? How can you tell? If you were able to hear this person speak you would hear only one side of the conversation. In what sense does the person hear the other side of the conversation?*

# What kind of God do we believe in?

## God is holy

Light is a symbol which is used to describe God. It points to God's glory or holiness. The word 'holy' describes God's perfect nature. Christians believe that God made people and God wants them to be holy too. This is why God has said that there is a right way to live. God has set holy standards, not to make life miserable and hard but to allow love and happiness to grow. The Christian way of life is called holiness. A Christian is made whole by knowing God.

## God is Trinity

We believe in one God who reveals himself in three distinct persons: as the Father who created the world, as the Son who came to bring forgiveness and rescue humanity, and as the Holy Spirit who is the Spirit of God filling people with love, joy and peace and making them more like Christ. This belief that God is 'three-in-one' is called the Trinity.

We find a very early reference to this in the last words of Paul's second letter to the Corinthian Church: 'The grace of our Lord Jesus Christ, the love of God and the fellowship of the Holy Spirit be with you all' (2 Corinthians 13.13).

In our everyday experience we know of different things which at the same time can

## Christian beliefs about God

- **God created the universe.** He is involved with his world and is in constant interaction with it. The story of the Bible is the story of salvation history, of how God interacts with history to save his people.

- **God is unique.**

  *God is everywhere* (omnipresent). The Bible teaches that there is nowhere outside his presence (Psalm 139.7–12).

  *God is all-powerful* (omnipotent). God will judge all people and will overcome all forces of darkness in the world.

  *God knows everything* (omniscient). He can see the past, present and future. God fully understands people's needs and secret thoughts (Psalm 139.1–6).

  *God is above space and time* (eternal, unchanging). God has always existed and owes his existence to no one (Isaiah 44.6).

→ *page 7*

be one. For example, water, ice and steam are different ways of being H$_2$O. The same person can be a mother, a cousin and a sister all at the same time.

**How are the three persons of the Trinity represented here? What message do you think the painter Dürer is trying to give?**

But what do we mean when we say that God is One in three persons? The Latin word *persona* (way of being) referred to an actor's mask which was changed with each role he played. The belief in God as Trinity is saying 'we believe in one God who exists and works in three ways'. Christians experience God in three distinct personal ways.

The doctrine of the Trinity means that in his own being God is a sort of communion of persons, eternally linked by love. Father, Son and Holy Spirit are eternally united by love, and scripture says that 'God is love' (1 John 4.8). That is why when we truly love others, then we are most like God.

## A creator God

James Weldon Johnson describes the creation of the world in a poem:

> And God stepped out on space,
> And he looked around and said:
> I'm lonely –
> I'll make me a world . . .

We believe that God created the world out of love and that evidence of his creating can be found in the beauty and detail of nature.

> God is the sea in which I swim, the atmosphere in which I breathe, the reality in which I move. I cannot find the tiniest thing which does not speak to me of Him, which is not somehow his image, His message, His call, His smile.
>
> (Carlo Carretto, *Love is for Living*)

# But what about suffering?

The existence of suffering in the world is the greatest obstacle for people believing in a loving God. How do you explain the belief in God in the face of so much suffering?

Christians have debated this question down the centuries. In one sense suffering is a mystery. When Job questioned God about the existence of suffering, God asked him: 'Who are you to question my wisdom with your ignorant empty words?' (Job 38.2).

One partial answer to the problem of suffering is to recognize that a lot of it can be traced to the fact that people have rebelled against God's wishes for them. Suffering is the result of their sin – their hatred of each other, their thoughtlessness towards the environment and the animal world. Not all suffering, however, is due to human sin.

Another answer is to explore the nature of God, to ask: 'Would it help if God intervened every time someone was suffering?' In his book *Why Do People Suffer?* James Jones recalls an incident from his own life. As you read it, imagine that the father is God and the child is each of us in our suffering.

*I remember once walking past the school at the end of our road. On the other side of the six-foot wall I could hear a small child crying inconsolably. A teacher was trying to comfort her but with little immediate success. Like any parent, the sound of a child sobbing stirred my heart.*

*As I walked on down the road, the child's crying ringing in my ears, I stopped dead in my tracks as I realized that the child who was in tears was my own daughter. Part of me wanted to vault over the wall and rescue her – to tell her that it was all right, that Daddy was here and she'd be OK now. But*

---

### . . . more Christian beliefs about God

- God is greater than words can describe or than we can imagine. However, **we can know God through faith** – putting our trust in him.

- **God is holy and wants people to be holy like himself. The word 'holy' describes God's perfect nature.** God sets holy standards for people to live up to – like the Ten Commandments.

- **The Bible uses a number of word pictures to describe different attributes of God.** God is likened to a shepherd (Psalm 23), a rock, shield and fortress (Psalm 18.2), a judge (1 Samuel 2.3), a king (Jeremiah 10.7).

- **God reveals himself in a number of ways.** God shows people what he is like through his actions in history (Isaiah 41.1–4):
  - God reveals himself in the Bible (2 Peter 1.19–21);
  - God reveals himself through creation (Psalm 19.1–4; Romans 1.20);
  - God revealed himself fully in Jesus. Jesus' life and teaching showed people what God was truly like. Jesus is sometimes described as the human window into God. Jesus said: 'Whoever has seen me has seen the Father' (John 14.9).

- **God makes covenants (agreements) with people.** He makes promises to humanity, and although people break their promises to God he is faithful in keeping his. God is like the loving and forgiving father in the parable of the Prodigal Son (Luke 15). God is pictured as a generous lover in Hosea: in spite of people disobeying him and his laws he still loves them.

- Although God is often referred to in the masculine, **Christians do not believe in a male concept of God.** In the Bible God is likened to both a father (Deuteronomy 1.31) and a mother (Isaiah 49.15).

- God is one being but is also three persons: Father, Son and Holy Spirit, who are all equally God. This belief is known as the **Trinity – the belief that God is Three in One.**

*another part of me knew that I should do nothing of the kind – that I had to leave her so that others could come near to her and help her.*

In the end, there is no answer to the problem of suffering which will fully satisfy our reason. Perhaps the most important thing to say is that as Christians we do not believe that God wills our suffering. He does not sit on a throne far away, deciding which of us will suffer today. On the contrary, the Cross of Jesus means that God himself shares our suffering. He suffers alongside us. (See Chapter 4, 'Jesus: Death & Resurrection'.)

## THINKING IT THROUGH

- ⧖ Think about how you came to believe in God. What evidence is there of God's presence in the world?

- ⧖ What do you understand prayer to be? Does God answer prayers? In what sense does God answer prayers?

- ⧖ Does James Jones' account of the father and his child help you to believe in a loving God in the face of suffering?

## BIBLE STUDY

**Read the following descriptions of God in the Bible:**

> Deuteronomy 32.6,10
>
> Isaiah 49.14–15
>
> Psalm 18.2
>
> 1 Timothy 6.15
>
> 1 Corinthians 4.5

- ◆ **Is God described in terms of gender (i.e. male or female)? What does this say about God?**

- ◆ **What do these descriptions say about God's relationship to people?**

## FOR PRAYER & REFLECTION

*God be in my head*
*and in my understanding.*
*God be in my eyes*
*and in my looking.*
*God be in my mouth*
*and in my speaking.*
*God be in my heart*
*and in my thinking.*
*God be at mine end*
*and at my departing.*

### SOME PRAYER TOPICS . . .

- ❖ A prayer of thanks for all the good things God has created.

- ❖ To say sorry for all the times when you have turned away from God and God's will for your life.

- ❖ To ask God to come into the situation you find yourself in at the moment – to ask for God's help, protection and guidance.

## A beautiful world often spoiled

The end of the twentieth century has seen the best and worst of human nature – humanity displayed in its extreme forms. Human beings have put men on the moon, and have achieved a medical revolution which includes heart transplants and antibiotics which can banish bacterial infection. Smallpox has virtually disappeared from the planet, along with many other infectious diseases. We can travel from Britain to the USA in three hours and instant communication has created the impression, if not the reality, of a 'global village'.

But the past century has also seen the devastation of the First World War, which reduced much of northern France and Belgium to mud and burnt tree stumps and cost the lives of hundreds of thousands of young men – barely a village in Britain lacks a memorial to their sacrifice. This was followed by the loss of at least 50 million lives in Stalin's purges, the Jewish Holocaust, the nuclear bombing of Hiroshima and Nagasaki, and the rest of the destruction brought about by the Second World War. The napalm bombing of Vietnam, the slaughter following the cultural revolution in

China in the 1960s, the Killing Fields of Cambodia and 'ethnic cleansing' in what was Yugoslavia offer no more reassuring a picture of human nature.

So, this century is unique in the scale of both human misery and achievement. Human beings have enjoyed greater prosperity and stability in the rich countries than ever before but wars and starvation have also exposed countless millions to unprecedented suffering.

The good aspects of life give us hope but the extent of evil in the world disturbs us. Evil threatens our happiness and security. Thousands of innocent shoppers can be walking around a shopping mall on a Saturday afternoon feeling perfectly secure. Moments later an exploding bomb has injured and killed many of them and destroyed the shops and the livelihoods of those who work in them.

Experiences like this can make us feel that human beings have missed the

*Throughout history and especially in the twentieth century, evil has broken up whole communities and turned innocent people into refugees. Why do people do this to each other?*

# Christian beliefs about human nature and sin

- Although many do not take it as literal history, the story of Adam and Eve expresses deep Christian truths about human nature and sin. It is a description of how we are now, and not of how we came to be this way. According to the story, Adam and Eve were placed in the Garden of Eden after they were created and had everything they needed. There was no shortage of food and they got on in complete harmony with all the other creatures. They were without self-consciousness and so they walked about the Garden naked but without embarrassment, like very young children running naked around a sandy beach on a warm day. But they were given one command: they were forbidden to eat of the Tree of the Knowledge of Good and Evil. However, the serpent told Eve to ignore this command and Eve gave in to temptation and took fruit from this tree and tempted Adam to share it with her. By this disobedience, they 'fell' from the harmonious relationship which they had with God. So, this story is called 'The Fall Story' and their sin is called original sin because it goes back to the origins of humanity.

- The Bible lists the worst consequences of the Fall. Adam and Eve were banished from the Garden of Eden to a life of labour ending in death and Eve was to suffer pain in childbirth. They lost harmony with the natural world, which is symbolized by the fear and hatred which comes about between them and the serpent. Their son, Cain, committed the first murder by killing his brother, Abel. Death, suffering, crime and war remain the experiences of life which trouble us most.

- This story paints a clear picture of the way that human beings have a capacity for the misuse of their free will but also that death and pain are not what human beings were ultimately created for. Adam and Eve started out in a world free from them.

- In fact, the Bible shows how God made human beings and the whole creation as something good and as something which he loved and approved of. Human beings are made in the image of God. This means that we were created good and are, by nature, closer to God than anything else in the Creation. On a lesser scale, we are creators, as the arts, sciences and human society itself show.

➔ page 12

mark, that we have fallen short of what we could be. We are like a marksman or archer aiming for a bullseye and missing the target.

Christians call this sense of falling short sin. Individual actions that make us fall short are 'sins'.

# What is sin?

At the heart of sin lies 'I'. Sin is **selfish**.

We can easily sin by putting ourselves first and ignoring others. The story below is adapted from *The Brothers Karamazov* by Dostoevsky:

### THE WICKED WOMAN AND THE ONION

*There was once a very wicked woman who died and went to hell. Her guardian angel took pity on her and asked God whether there was anything that could be done to rescue her. God told the angel that he should search the record of her life for any good deed which she might have done. If he could find one, this could be used to save her. The angel went away and searched through the Book of Life and could not find anything to begin with. Eventually, though, he found one kind act. One day, a beggar had come to the woman asking for food. She had gone into her garden and pulled up an onion which she had given to the beggar. The angel returned to God and told him this. God then told the angel to go to the lake of fire and lift the woman out with the help of the onion. The angel went to the lake and called, 'Woman, woman.' She* came swimming across the lake of fire and, clasping onto the onion, was lifted from the fire. As this happened, others saw what was happening and they too were lifted from the lake by holding on to her feet and long skirt. For a moment, the wicked woman and several other people were being lifted from the lake. But then she felt the tugging of the other people on her feet and on her skirt. Looking down on them, she kicked them away from her. At that moment, the onion leaves which were supporting her snapped and she and all the others fell back into the lake of fire, where they are to this day. The angel went away and wept.

In a word, the woman's selfishness spoils everything. Her selfishness means that not only she but many others lose the chance of rescue.

Sin is like a poison, as this story shows:

A man went to see his doctor because he had three nasty boils. He asked the doctor to remove each of them. The doctor replied that there was no point in just treating these surface symptoms. There was a poison which had spread all over the man's body. Only when this had been treated would the boils go . . .

The human race is sick and has 'boils' which affect it – think of the suffering caused by war and the lack of food. We would love to 'cut them out' but we will never succeed unless we recognize the 'poison within us' which causes them.

(Michael Ramsey, Introducing the Christian Faith, adapted).

Sin **spreads** like a disease. Think of the way bullying spreads in a school. Once there have been one or two incidents of bullying which have gone unstopped, others copy and bullying becomes a way of life.

Abuse of the environment – as well as of human communities – is an aspect of sin.

Christians believe that sin may affect all aspects of life. For example, human neglect can cause disease and natural disasters. The whole world, therefore, needs saving. This is why the gospels show Jesus restoring the sick to health and calming the storm. These stories show the way in which God can reverse the sin and disorder of every aspect of the world.

. . . your iniquities have been barriers between you and your God, and your sins have hidden his face from you so that he does not hear (Isaiah 59).

Sin **separates** us from those whom we love and from God, as this true story shows:

In America, two brothers convicted of murder both offered to donate a kidney to their mother before they were executed.

She had raised nine other children successfully but her two youngest, aged 29 and 28, had a long history of wrongdoing. They drank heavily, took drugs and got into trouble with the police from an early age. The younger of the two was convicted of rape at the age of 16 and spent two years in a juvenile detention centre and seven in prison.

In 1992, the two brothers and their cousin lured a 64-year-old man from a bar with a promise of more drinks at another bar. Afterwards, the man was found beaten to death. All three were convicted of first-degree murder and sentenced to death.

→ page 12

## ... more Christian beliefs about human nature and sin

● **This closeness between God and Man is spoilt by human disobedience but God doesn't leave it there.** God made promises (covenants) with Noah, Abraham and Moses, to whom he also gave laws, assuring them of his favour as long as they and their people obeyed his will. Often they failed, so God sent prophets to remind them of their promises. Finally, he sent Jesus to achieve reconciliation between God and Man, the atonement (at-one-ment) (see Chapter 4: 'Jesus: Death & Resurrection' for more about this). The fact that God went on trying to restore relations between God and human beings shows how important they are to God and how much God wants them to make something of their lives.

● **But we are unable to be good or save ourselves just because we want to.** However hard we try, we cannot rid our own lives or society of death, suffering, crime and war, or any of the other things which spoil our lives. God has had to take the initiative in helping us.

● **We need someone to help us: we need a Saviour.** We may make progress in organizing society, through better health services, better food and housing, and better education, but we never quite succeed. The twentieth century, which saw the greatest improvement in the quality of life in Britain and other 'rich' countries, saw the greatest scale of war, destruction and starvation as well.

● **Jesus in his life and death restored human nature.** In the New Testament we learn how Jesus lived and how he wants us to live. We also discover how he defeated death and evil by dying on the Cross and being raised to new life by God. He opens up the possibility of a new kind of human life. Our old fallen nature can be restored to its full potential.

● **We can share in what Jesus did. By becoming a Christian, death and suffering will have no final power over us.** Jesus taught that all who followed him will suffer and die but that they will also be given new life.

● **Jesus' work in restoring human beings to the fullness of life which God intended is not over yet.** There is still enormous suffering and evil in the world and individual Christians continue to sin even after they have turned to Christ. They need the help of Jesus and other Christians, which they experience in worship and prayer, to help to bring about the full reign of Jesus on earth and in heaven, what Christians call the Kingdom of God. This will not be completed until Christ returns. The whole process, as St Paul says, is like a woman in labour, where suffering and struggle have to come before the birth of a new life.

*Meanwhile, their mother's kidney disease had worsened and she was receiving dialysis to clean her blood three times a week. This meant hours attached to a machine, persistent poor health and the prospect of living only a little time longer. Doctors said her best chance lay with a transplant if the right donor could be found.*

*On death row, the younger brother offered a kidney to give his mother the chance to live. So did the elder brother when she went to visit him later. He told her that she should have asked him first. Doctors tested both brothers to see whether their kidneys were suitable for transplant. Even though the younger of the two had been the first to offer, his kidney wasn't compatible. Fortunately, his elder brother's was and their mother soon had a successful transplant at a hospital in Philadelphia.*

*The younger brother was executed by lethal injection in March 1996. At the time of writing, his elder brother, who had donated a kidney, was waiting for the date of his execution to be set. The mother of*

*People are imprisoned by sin but some good part of their human nature may remain.*

*these two young men is delighted with her recovery but broken-hearted about her sons.*

This story shows how sin **separates**. It separated the two sons from ever living a normal life again. However, the story also shows that the good part of human nature is never completely lost even in people who have committed the worst sins. These boys were still capable of making sacrifices to show their love for their mother.

## THINKING IT THROUGH

⧗ Are some sins worse than others? What do you think?

⧗ Does it help to see sin as a sickness? If sin is sickness, what is health?

⧗ Discuss how this sickness affects:
(a) the world;
(b) your neighbourhood;
(c) yourself.

⧗ Why do you think that some people do wrong from an early age?

⧗ Do you think that anyone is 'all bad'?

⧗ How good are most people? Are some people wholly good – do you know anyone?

## BIBLE STUDY

God's love will save the whole creation.

Find Chapter 8 of the first letter of Paul to the Romans.

Reflect on these parts:

♦ How can the Spirit help us? (verses 5–9).

♦ How close can we be to God?

How should we feel about suffering? (verses 13–18).

♦ How does this describe sin as affecting the whole creation?

What hope does it hold out to us? (verses 19–22).

## FOR PRAYER & REFLECTION

*A prayer asking for protection from sin and danger:*

*Almighty and everlasting Father,*
*we thank you that you have brought us*
*safely to the beginning of this day.*
*Keep us from falling into sin*
*or running into danger;*
*order us in all our doings;*
*and guide us to do always*
*what is right in your eyes;*
*through Jesus Christ our Lord.*

*Amen.*

## *S*OME PRAYER TOPICS . . .

❖ For help with overcoming selfishness.

❖ That the world can be delivered from the sin which spoils it, especially war and the destruction of the environment.

❖ For the strength to say 'no' to the sin which spreads through our lives.

❖ That we should not be separated by sin from one another.

# *J*ESUS: LIFE & MINISTRY

*'Do you believe and trust in his Son Jesus Christ?'*

**'I believe in Jesus Christ, his only Son, our Lord . . .'**

Today more people follow Jesus Christ than anyone else on earth. Jesus' influence can be seen in the paintings in this chapter. Throughout the centuries artists have painted Jesus in ways which make sense to them. In China Jesus is shown as Chinese; in Ethiopia he is painted as an Ethiopian. All cultures and centuries have been influenced by Jesus Christ. But who is Jesus?

*He was born in an obscure village, the child of a peasant woman.*

*He grew up in still another village, where he worked in a carpenter's shop until he was 30.*

*Then for three years he was an itinerant preacher.*

*He never wrote a book.*

*He never held an office.*

*He never had a family or owned a house.*

*He didn't go to college. He never travelled 200 miles from the place where he was born.*

*He did none of the things one usually associates with greatness.*

*He had no credentials but himself.*

*He was only 33 when public opinion turned against him. His friends ran away.*

*He was turned over to his enemies and went through the mockery of a trial.*

*He was nailed to a cross between two thieves.*

*While he was dying, his executioners gambled for his clothing, the only property he had on earth.*

*When he was dead, he was laid in a borrowed grave through the pity of a friend.*

**Look through the paintings of Jesus in this chapter. The image above comes from the island of Goa, India. Why do you think artists from different countries have chosen to depict Jesus as though he were a member of their own community?**

*Nineteen centuries have come and gone, and today he is the central figure of the human race, the leader of mankind's progress.*

*All the armies that ever marched,*

*all the navies that ever sailed,*

*all the parliaments that ever sat,*

*all the kings that ever reigned,*

*put together, have not affected*

*the life of man on earth*

*as much as that*

*One Solitary Life.*

# Who was Jesus?

## A human being like us

Jesus was a man who walked the dusty streets, was tempted, as all people are, and died a physical death as a criminal on a cross. But in his teaching people recognized that he spoke with an authority unlike anyone else. In his miracles they saw a supernatural power at work in him. Jesus was not an 'ordinary' man, but he was still fully a human being. He shows the true potential of our human nature when it is perfectly united with God.

## The Son of God

During his life Jesus would often go away to a quiet place to be alone with God. These times of quietness were the source of his inner strength. Jesus spoke of the special relationship which he had with God, whom he called 'Father'. According to John's Gospel, he identified himself with God the Father, telling his disciples that 'The Father and I are one' (John 10.30) and that 'if you know me you would know my Father also' (John 8.19).

As the early disciples thought about the life of Jesus they came to believe that he was more than a human being. He was God's Son who came and lived as a man on earth. Matthew gave Jesus the name 'Emmanuel', which means 'God is with us'. The early Church came to refer to this belief as the *Incarnation*. The word means 'in the flesh', and refers to the belief that God became a human being in Jesus.

**This mosaic of Jesus with St Minias comes from San Miniato al Monte in Florence. Does it show the human or the divine person of Jesus? How can you tell?**

John's Gospel begins with a poem describing the Incarnation (*NRSV*, John 1.1–5,14–18). In describing Jesus as the *Word* of God, St John is telling us that he is God's ultimate *self-expression* in human terms.

*In the beginning was the Word, and the Word was with God, and the Word was God. He was in the beginning with God. All things came into being through him, and without him not one thing came into being. What has come into being in him was life, and the life was the light of all people. The light shines in the darkness, and the darkness did not overcome it . . .*

*And the Word became flesh and lived among us, and we have seen his glory, the glory as of a father's only son, full of grace and truth. (John testified to him and cried out, 'This was he of whom I said, "He who comes after me ranks ahead of me because he was before me."') From his fullness we have all received, grace upon grace. The law indeed was given through Moses; grace and truth came through Jesus Christ. No one has ever seen God. It is God the only Son who is close to the Father's heart, who has made him known.*

## Christian beliefs about Jesus

- **Jesus was a historical person who lived in the first century** AD. In addition to the four gospel accounts of his life (written between 30 and 60 years after Jesus' crucifixion) both Jewish (namely, Josephus) and Roman historians (Tacitus, Pliny and Suetonius) record his existence.

- **Jesus was Jewish.** He was brought up within a Jewish family which took great care to observe the commandments.

- **The word 'Jesus' (Hebrew 'Joshua') means 'God saves' or 'God rescues'.** Christians believe that Jesus was sent by God to save and rescue people. The gospel writers show that Jesus was special in a number of ways. They tell us *his birth* was heralded by angels (Luke 1.26–38; 2.8–14); God spoke to Joseph about the birth in dreams (Matthew 1.20–24; 2.13); it was a virgin birth (by the power of the Holy Spirit, Matthew 1.23). When he was 30 years old he was *baptized* by his cousin John in the River Jordan. At his baptism he heard a voice saying: 'You are my own dear Son. I am pleased with you,' (Mark 1.11). Towards the end of his life God spoke again through a cloud at Jesus' *transfiguration* ('This is my own dear Son – listen to him,' Mark 9.2–13).

- **Jesus was the Messiah whom the Jews had been eagerly waiting for.** At the time of Jesus the Jews were eagerly waiting for God to send the Messiah who would rescue them from their Roman oppressors. Jesus' closest disciples came to believe that Jesus was the Messiah (Luke 9.20). Jesus himself said he was the Christ (Mark 14.62). But Jesus taught that he was not interested in earthly power. Instead of saving them from Roman rule he had come to save them from their sinful ways and to bring people back to oneness with God. However, Jesus taught that he had not only come for the Jews but for all people. Christians today call Jesus 'Christ', which is the Greek word for Messiah.

➔ page 18

# The coming of God's kingdom changes the world

Jesus summed up his message by proclaiming at the beginning of his ministry, 'The right time has come . . . and the Kingdom of God is near! Turn away from your sins and believe the Good News!' (Mark 1.15). By the term 'Kingdom of God' he did not mean a place but, instead, the reign of God. He called people to follow him and to accept God as king of their lives. He does the same to us today.

But what did the reign of God mean? What sort of kingdom was Jesus bringing in? He gave a clear description of it when he spoke in the synagogue at Nazareth after his baptism. He read the following passage from the book of Isaiah:

> 'The spirit of the Lord is upon me,
> because he has anointed me
> to bring good news to the poor.
> He has sent me to proclaim release
> to the captives
> and recovery of sight to the blind,
> to let the oppressed go free,
> to proclaim the year of the Lord's favour.'

And he rolled up the scroll, gave it back to the attendant, and sat down. The eyes of all in the synagogue were fixed on him. Then he began to say to them, 'Today this scripture has been fulfilled in your hearing' (NRSV, Luke 4.18–21).

Then he made the startling announcement that this scripture was being fulfilled in their presence: Jesus himself was bringing in God's kingdom rule over people's lives and over all the earth. God's rule over the earth would be good news for the poor and the downtrodden. God would fight on the side of justice and peace. Jesus had come to bring God's love to all people, especially those despised by society.

In the gospels Jesus is often seen mixing with the outcasts of society (lepers, prostitutes, the poor). He came to show God's love for them.

Christians today continue to be called to follow Jesus in bringing about justice in the world. Many work alongside charities (both local and international) which seek to help people who are often ignored by the rest of society.

AL TERCER DIA DE SUFRIMIENTOS CUANDO SE CREA TODO CONSUMADO HA DE VOLVER Y NO PODRAN MATARLO !

*This image of Jesus as a person who fought for justice is very popular today in churches in Latin America, where there is a great gulf between the rich and the poor. If this picture had a caption, what do you think it would say?*

## Jesus the teacher

When Jesus taught about the kingdom of God he spoke with an authority which amazed people. His words had a power all of their own. He spoke of a God of love who taught that the greatest command was to love God with all your heart, soul, mind and strength and to love your neighbour as you love

*This picture of Jesus the teacher comes from China. What can you see in this painting?*

yourself (Mark 12.28–34). He likened God to a father who accepted a wayward son back into his loving arms, to a shepherd who went in search of the one lost sheep and to a woman who searched diligently for a lost coin and rejoiced when she found it (Luke 15).

## . . . more Christian beliefs about Jesus

- **Jesus came to bring in the Kingdom of God.** Jesus summed up his message with the words: 'The right time has come, and the Kingdom of God is near! Turn away from your sins and believe the Good News' (Mark 1.15). Jews understood the phrase 'Kingdom of God' to mean not a place but a state of accepting God as King of your life. In his teaching he showed that the Kingdom was already present in the lives of those people who had accepted God as ruler of their life. But the Kingdom was like a small mustard seed which had to grow into a large plant (Mark 4.30–32). The Kingdom of God would grow likewise. In Jesus' miracles God's Kingdom was being established in Jesus' ministry of casting out evil spirits, healing ill people, raising people from the dead and showing God's authority even over nature.

- **Jesus was fully human.** One of the favourite ways Jesus spoke about himself was to use the title 'Son of Man'. This is a Hebrew expression which means 'the human being'. He saw himself as a Jewish man who was called to be obedient to God. He openly declared that 'I do nothing on my own authority, but I say only what the Father has instructed me to say' (John 8.28).

- **Jesus was fully divine.** For Christians Jesus is more than a good man. They believe he is the Son of God. This belief is called 'incarnation' – God 'became a human being and, full of grace and truth, lived among us' (John 1.14). Jesus often spoke of the special relationship he had with God. He calls himself Son (Matthew 11.27). Christians believe that Jesus is the second person of the Trinity (God the Father, Son and Holy Spirit).

➜ *page 20*

Jesus often taught in everyday stories called parables. His teaching has a power to change people's lives today, as Robert Van de Weyer experienced in his own life.

*On Christmas Day, 1970, Robert Van de Weyer wrote in his diary: 'I have decided to try an experiment: to make Jesus my teacher for a test period of six months. During this time I shall act as a full disciple, studying his teachings closely and following them as far as I can. Then on June 25th next year I shall stand back and review what has happened to me.' During the next few months Robert discovered that his unbelief in God started to give way. For example, on 9 February, 1971, just six weeks into his experiment he wrote:*

*'As I try to follow Jesus' instructions my agnosticism is beginning to waver. When I am angry or depressed or in any other unloving mood, I make myself say little prayers asking for help to overcome the mood. I do this because Jesus instructs me to. To my surprise I am generally finding the prayer works, and my bad mood quickly disappears . . . I also have the strong impression of an outside force working within me. It seems to demand my submission, and having submitted to it I feel I have no control over it . . . I am also now aware of the force each evening as I say the Lord's Prayer when I reach the phrase "thy will be done". As I turn the phrase over in my mind I sense the presence of a will greater than my own, pressing upon me.'*

## Jesus the miracle worker

Jesus not only spoke about God's kingly rule, he also demonstrated it in his miracles. He showed God's loving compassion towards people who were sick, and God's power over sickness, evil, nature and even death. Many people followed Jesus because of the miracles which he performed by the power of God's Holy Spirit. After he had died and been raised his apostles carried on his work. They also performed miracles, healing and restoring people to full health and rescuing them from all that oppressed them.

Christians believe that the power of Jesus to heal is still at work today. Some Christians, especially in the Charismatic or Pentecostal movement, still claim to experience miraculous healing, but often we experience the healing of spirit, soul and body gradually, as we grow closer to God in prayer and the sacraments. (See Chapter 18 on the sacrament of anointing the sick.)

*Jesus brought in God's kingdom by his words and his actions. As in this picture, taken from an Ethiopian Bible, he healed many people. We believe that Jesus heals people today. Many churches have a ministry of healing.*

# Jesus – a window into God

Jesus often spoke of the special relationship he had with God. He told his followers that 'The Father and I are one.' In John's Gospel Jesus uses seven sayings to describe himself. They all start with the words 'I am':

- *I am the bread of life. He who comes to me will never be hungry; he who believes in me will never be thirsty (John 6.35).*

- *I am the light of the world. Whoever follows me will have the light of life and will never walk in darkness (John 8.12).*

- *I am the gate for the sheep . . . Whoever comes in by me will be saved (John 10.7,9).*

- *I am the good shepherd who is willing to die for the sheep (John 10.11).*

- *I am the resurrection and the life (John 11.25).*

- *I am the way, the truth, and the life: no one goes to the Father except by me (John 14.6).*

- *I am the real vine, and my Father is the gardener (John 15.1).*

Jesus was no ordinary man. Jesus points the way to God, he is the Son of God, who gives meaning and purpose to our lives.

Joe Gibbs, famous in Washington as senior coach of the Redskins football team, said:

> *A lot of people in the world would probably look at me and say: 'Man, if I could just coach in the Super Bowl, I'd be happy and fulfilled . . .' But I'm here to tell you, it takes something else in your life besides money, position, football, power and fame. The vacuum in each of our lives can only be filled through a personal relationship with our Lord and Saviour Jesus Christ. Otherwise, I'm telling you, we'll spend the rest of our lives in a meaningless existence. I've seen it in football players' eyes, and I've seen it in men who are on their death bed. There's nothing else that will fill that vacuum.*
>
> (Charles Colson, *The Body*)

## Jesus – God in the flesh (the Incarnation)

In the thirteenth century Elizabeth was Queen of Hungary. Although she was a wealthy woman she did not forget those who had little. Many were poor because of a famine which had hit the land. She spent an enormous amount of money on building hospitals, giving money to the poor and providing homes for orphans. Tragedy hit Elizabeth's life when her husband died in a war. The courtiers in the palace took advantage of this to demand that Elizabeth justify

---

### *. . . more Christian beliefs about Jesus*

● **Jesus shows us what God is like.** When God became a human being in Jesus he showed us God's amazing love for us by coming 'down to our level', to help us and to save us. In the Gospels Jesus is shown as someone who really cares about those who are rejected by society (at the time of Jesus these included Samaritans, tax collectors, lepers, the poor and prostitutes). We are called to follow Jesus' example (Philippians 2.5).

● **Jesus' death and resurrection were the key events in his life.** Through his death it has been possible for us to be at one with God again. His resurrection gives us hope that death is not the end, that good triumphs over evil and that our destiny is to be with God for ever.

---

giving away her royal money to the poor. They were themselves greedy and had no interest in the poor or in Elizabeth's Christian beliefs. Elizabeth was forced to make a decision between the poor and her royalty. She chose the poor and decided to sacrifice her wealth, power and even her family ties for them. She sacrificed the comfort and richness of her palace to live in the cold and damp conditions of the poor. She worked for them day and night: feeding, nursing and loving them. Elizabeth died young, at 24. Her decision to leave the royal life and live with the poor contributed to her death. However, they were worth it – she loved them.

This historical example is a word picture of what God did when he became human in the person of Jesus – it was a costly thing to do. St Paul expressed this belief in his letter to the Philippians:

> *Christ Jesus . . . always had the nature of God,*
> *but he did not think that by force he should try to become equal with God.*
> *Instead of this, of his own free will he gave up all he had,*
> *and took the nature of a servant.*
> *He became like man and appeared in human likeness.*
> *He was humble and walked the path of obedience all the way to death – his death on the cross.*
>
> (Philippians 2.5–8)

*What difference does it make that God became a man in Jesus? It makes a great difference to our understanding of God – now God is near.* (David Edwards)

## THINKING IT THROUGH

⧗ Discuss what you think Jesus meant by each of his 'I am' sayings.

⧗ What do you think of the following argument?

*I am trying here to prevent anyone saying the really foolish thing that people often say about Him: 'I'm ready to accept Jesus as a great moral teacher, but I don't accept His claim to be God.' That is the one thing we must not say. A man who was merely a man and said the sort of things Jesus said would not be a great moral teacher. He would either be a lunatic – on a level with the man who says he is a poached egg – or else he would be the Devil of Hell. You must make your choice. Either this man was, and is, the Son of God: or else a madman or something worse.*

(C. S. Lewis, *Mere Christianity*)

## BIBLE STUDY

Read the account of Jesus' meeting with the man who was blind from birth (John 9).

As you read this passage you will find that people's reactions to Jesus change throughout the story. This account compares two forms of blindness – physical blindness and spiritual blindness.

- ◆ How did Jesus heal the blind man? (verses 6–7).
- ◆ How does the blind man's description of Jesus change throughout the story? (verses 11, 17, 33, 38).
- ◆ How does the Pharisees' description of Jesus change as the story progresses? (verses 16, 24).

**Max Beckmann's 'Christ and the woman taken in adultery' is a modern representation of the way Jesus showed love and forgiveness to the outcasts in society. Read the story for yourself in John 8.1–11.**

## FOR PRAYER & REFLECTION

*All praise to you,*
*almighty God and heavenly King,*
*who sent your Son into the world*
*to take our nature upon him*
*and to be born of a pure virgin:*
*grant that, as we are born again in him,*
*so he may continually dwell in us*
*and reign on earth as he reigns in heaven,*
*now and for ever.*

### SOME PRAYER TOPICS . . .

❖ That more people can hear the good news about Jesus.

❖ For Jesus' spirit to live within us.

❖ For courage to live out Jesus' teaching.

# *J*ESUS: DEATH & RESURRECTION

Whether it's River Phoenix, Princess Diana or Gandhi, we are interested in the way people die. We see it as fitting their lives. Some deaths have a power of their own. Some people even become famous because of the way they die. Often this is the case with heroes and heroines: their death sums up their life. This is certainly true in the case of Jesus. The gospel writers present Jesus' death as the climax of his life. They devote more pages of their books to his death than to any other part of his life. In St John's Gospel,  Jesus himself points to his death as the fulfilment of his life. One of the last words he says from the cross is 'It is finished' ('It is accomplished'). But why was his death so important?

*If you look carefully, you will see that the cross is like a drawn bow with an arrow. The cross is a sign of hope because the tortured body of Jesus is bound, so to speak, to an arrow pointing towards new life.*

## Why Jesus' death is important

Artists throughout the centuries have taken the death and resurrection of Jesus as their subject. They have done this because they believed that these events continued to have importance and were not simply something that had happened in the past to the historical Jesus.

Here is a painting from an altarpiece by Matthias Grünewald, painted between 1513 and 1515 for the chapel at the hospital for plague victims in the small village of Isenheim. Imagine the patients ill with the plague, with no modern drugs or painkillers and little chance of recovery. They would have wondered what was the point of their lives. They would have asked the questions which all people ask when confronted by suffering and death: 'How can God help?' and 'What does he know of human suffering like ours?'

The picture suggests two answers:

● On the altar they saw Christ, their God, with the same suppurating ulcers as their own. It would have helped them to believe that they were not left on their own. Jesus is the God-who-suffers-with-us.

● The altar panels on which the crucified Lord is depicted open up to show a picture of the resurrection. To the question 'How can God help?' comes the answer: the body which hung there dead on the cross, covered in ulcers, is transformed into the body which gives off a dazzling light – a splendour also in store for us.

# Why did Jesus have to die?

We believe that through his death Jesus mended the relationship between God and humanity. He made human beings and God to be 'at one'. This is known as the atonement ('at-one-ment').

The cross is a symbol of God's love for us. In Ephesians 3.16–19 Paul describes the extent of God's love. Of its length, depth and height, he writes:

● *how long is it?* it lasts all the way through a lifetime to eternity;

● *how deep is it?* it can reach down to you and me wherever we are, however much of a mess we have made of our lives;

● *how high is it?* it can lift us to the highest place of that relationship with God.

And if you look at these things – how wide, long, high and deep is the love of Christ, you will see that it forms the shape of the cross. It is on the cross that we see how much God loved us – so much that he was willing to send his Son to die for us.

## Jesus died as an atonement

The word 'atonement' means to make amends. We believe that through his death Jesus mended the broken relationship between God and humanity which had been caused by sin. Now God and humanity can freely communicate with each other. A picture at Catterick Camp, painted during the First World War, shows a signaller lying dead in no-man's-land. He had been sent out to repair a cable broken down by shellfire. There he lies, cold in death, but with his task accomplished; for beside him lies the rejoined section of cable. Beneath the picture stands one pregnant word – 'THROUGH'.

On the cross Jesus put himself in our place. The basic thing which is wrong with human beings is our separation from God. On the cross Jesus cried out the terrifying words, 'My God, why have you forsaken me?' Although he was the Son of God, on the cross Jesus shared the pain and terror of our lostness. He came to be where we are, in order to bring us back into his own relationship of union with the Father.

**THROUGH**

## In Jesus God takes our place on the cross

Maria Skobtsova was a Russian nun who lived in Paris. When the Germans occupied the city she felt God was calling her to the risky mission of feeding and hiding Jews. She realized that this could easily lead to her imprisonment and death. She wrote that 'each of us is called to follow Christ and give himself for his friends'. All went well for a month. Hundreds of Jews were hidden by her in the convent and many escaped. However, at the end of the month the Gestapo came. Mother Maria was sent to Ravensbruck concentration camp.

At the camp the German guards came to refer to her as 'that wonderful Russian nun'. Many sensed the presence of God in her. She spent two and a half years in the camp. Then one day a group of women were lined up outside a building for baths. One woman became hysterical. Calmly, Mother Maria took her place in the line and became her substitute. She passed through the doors. She had entered the gas chambers. It was Good Friday, 1945.

*When Jesus rose from the dead he broke the chains of death. The power of the Devil was broken. This picture comes from Panama.*

Maria Skobtsova died in the place of the scared woman about to be killed. So also we believe that people deserve to die for all their sin against God, but instead in Jesus God died in our place because he loves us.

## Jesus defeated Satan

Placing Jesus on the cross would have made it appear that evil had defeated good. However, the resurrection reverses this and demonstrates Christ's victory over evil – Jesus went through death to new resurrected life. Satan and the powers of darkness could not hold Jesus in the grave.

## Jesus died as a sacrifice for us

We can use the word 'sacrifice' to explain his death: Jesus did not resist his death – he went as a willing sacrifice, as a soldier sacrifices his life in order that victory may be possible. Jesus wanted to show us how much he loved us – it was a costly sacrifice. The Bible describes it by saying: 'For God loved the world so much that he gave his only Son, so that everyone who believes in him may not die but have eternal life' (John 3.16).

An example of what it means to be a sacrifice is found in the life of Oscar Romero. During the 1970s many South American countries sacrificed human rights in the pursuit of economic success. Many Christians spoke out against this. It has been estimated that between 1968 and 1979 approximately

1,500 priests, nuns and active laypersons were arrested, kidnapped, interrogated, tortured, defamed, exiled or assassinated. Oscar Romero was Archbishop of Salvador in the late 1970s and pledged 'to let my blood be a seed of freedom and the sign that hope will soon be a reality'. He was assassinated while saying mass in his cathedral on 24 March 1980.

Oscar Romero was willing to sacrifice his life in order to show God's love for the poor. Since 1980 the church in San Salvador has grown in strength and numbers. In the same way Jesus wanted to show us how much he loved us – it was a costly sacrifice.

## Jesus died as a ransom

We believe that our lives are often like a hostage to the Devil – we have an inclination to do what is wrong. Kidnappers demand ransoms to free hostages. We believe that **Jesus was our ransom** – he paid the price to buy our freedom.

> *For the Son of Man came not to be served but to serve, and to give his life a ransom for many. (NRSV, Mark 10.45)*

# Jesus rose from the dead

We believe that Jesus' death was not the end of the story. Jesus rose from the dead and was seen by many. Although there is no description of the actual event of the Resurrection in the gospels, members of the early Church were convinced of it for three reasons:

- The tomb was empty.
- Jesus appeared to people after his death.
- They felt his presence among them.

The resurrection is proof that good is greater than evil, life is stronger than death, and love is stronger than hate. The resurrection appearances show Jesus still with the marks of suffering on his body.

The festival of **Easter** which celebrates both the death and resurrection of Jesus **is our central festival.** Not only does it celebrate what Jesus did for us by dying for us but it also celebrates the fact that death is not the end. Jesus rose from the dead and by his resurrection gave us hope that we shall also be resurrected from the dead. We use light as a symbol of this new life.

**We experience the results of the resurrection in our lives today.** One of the earliest Christians to experience the risen presence of Jesus was St Paul. His conversion is recorded three times in the Acts of the Apostles (9.1–19; 22.6–16; 26.12–18). Christians all over the world feel Jesus' presence in their lives.

> *The resurrection means that Jesus is still living. He is living in our lives today and gives us hope for tomorrow.*
>
> (Sam, 17)

# Jesus ascended into heaven

After 40 days the book of Acts says Jesus returned (ascended) to heaven. This is the Bible's way of telling us that although he is no longer bound by the limitations of ordinary existence, nevertheless he is still alive, and capable of being present to those who believe in him at all places and at all times.

## Christian beliefs about Jesus' death and resurrection

- **The cross is the central symbol for Christians.** In every church it will be displayed, sometimes bare and sometimes with the image of Jesus (a crucifix).

- **Jesus died by being nailed to a cross.** This was the normal method of execution for a criminal in the Roman Empire. Jesus was crucified at the age of 33 on the order of Pontius Pilate, the Roman governor, after a trial in the Jewish High Court. Jews today are in no way responsible for his death.

- We believe **that through Jesus' death humankind and God were brought together again.**

- The day on which Jesus died is called '**Good' Friday** because we believe that what Jesus accomplished was 'Good'. Through his death, Jesus showed us how much God loves us – enough to send his Son to die for us.

## THINKING IT THROUGH

⧗ We have given River Phoenix, Princess Diana and Gandhi as examples of people whose deaths made a great impression on the public. Think of some others and explain why they are important to you. You might choose famous people or those known to you personally.

⧗ Which of the approaches to the atonement (sacrifice, ransom, etc.) makes most sense to you? What are your reasons?

⧗ How do Christians remind themselves of Jesus' death and resurrection when they worship?

## BIBLE STUDY

Read the gospel accounts of the crucifixion of Jesus (Matthew 27.45–56; Mark 15.33–41; Luke 23.44–49; John 19.28–30).

Although the gospels have much in common, there are some distinct differences between the accounts, so read carefully.

- ◆ What did Jesus say from the cross? Discuss what these sayings mean.

- ◆ What elements in these accounts suggest that something more than an ordinary death was taking place? (Take note about what happened to the sky, etc.)

- ◆ How did people react to watching his death?

## FOR PRAYER & REFLECTION

*Lord of all life and power,*
*who through the mighty resurrection of your Son*
*overcame the old order of sin and death*
*to make all things new in him:*
*grant that we, being dead to sin*
*and alive to you in Jesus Christ,*
*may reign with him in glory;*
*to whom with you and the Holy Spirit*
*be praise and honour, glory and might,*
*now and in all eternity.*

## SOME PRAYER TOPICS . . .

❖ Thank God for the love he has shown us by sending his Son to die on the cross.

❖ Ask for forgiveness of our sins – for ways in which we deny God's love for us.

❖ Prayers of praise that God in Jesus has won the victory over evil, giving us all new life.

*'Do you believe and trust in the Holy Spirit?'*

**'I believe in the Holy Spirit . . .'**

## Christianity: a supernatural religion

Do you believe in the supernatural? Do you believe that there is a spiritual realm which infiltrates the earthly? Do you believe that God actually speaks to people today? Do you believe that God performs miracles today? Do you believe that people can completely change, for example from being a drug pusher to being a missionary?

Christians answer YES to each of these questions. Christianity is not just a set of beliefs, or a moral code. It is a supernatural religion. God did not just create the world in the beginning like some divine watchmaker and then sit back and let it tick away. He is actively involved in it. God's supernatural power is alive and well today in the form of the Holy Spirit and it is at work in people to change them.

*On the day of Pentecost the Holy Spirit came to the disciples in the form of tongues of fire and a great wind. Fire and wind are frequent Bible pictures of the Holy Spirit.*

# The power to change

Sometimes it is very difficult, if not impossible, to change bad habits of our own free will. However, when a person becomes a Christian he or she begins a new life. With the help of the Holy Spirit a self-centred life begins to change to a God-centred one. Old habits begin to change. Sometimes this can be quite dramatic, as the following story about Corrie Ten Boom illustrates.

*Water is another symbol often used for the Holy Spirit. Water washes people physically clean. The Holy Spirit is God's purifying power working in people's lives.*

Corrie was a Dutch woman who suffered under the Nazis in Ravensbruck concentration camp during the Second World War. One day after the war an ex-guard turned up at a church service where Corrie was preaching. He asked her to forgive him for all the murders he had committed.

*I stood there – I whose sins had again and again to be forgiven by God – and I could not forgive. I stood there with the coldness clutching my heart. 'Jesus help me!' I prayed silently. 'I can lift my hand. You supply the feeling.' And so I thrust my hand into the one stretched out to me. And as I did, an incredible thing took place. The current started in my shoulder, raced down my arm and this healing warmth seemed to flood my whole being. I had never known God's love so intensely as I did then.*
(Corrie Ten Boom, *Tramp for the Lord*)

Corrie was able to forgive because the power of God's Holy Spirit had given her the power to do so.

## God's miraculous power

The Bible tells us that the apostles travelled from town to town healing people by the power of God's Holy Spirit. Some people think that such events do not happen today. However, there are instances of healing which apparently cannot be accounted for in conventional medical terms. Also, there are many occasions where, although they may not recover physically, sick people have had their sense of inner, mental wholeness restored by prayer.

Susan Howatch explains this well: 'Christian healers make a distinction between a cure and a healing. Not everyone can be cured of whatever physical and mental illness afflicts them, but spiritual and emotional wounds can be healed so that a better quality of life is obtained.' She illustrates this in her novel *A Question of Integrity*, based on real life experience: 'Alice is interested in the people who go up to the altar for the laying on of hands and she's particularly interested in a stroke victim in a wheelchair. Alice sees that the stroke victim is not cured but in some mysterious way she's much healed because when the wheelchair comes back down the aisle after the laying on of hands the victim's face is radiant – her mood is quite changed.'

## THINKING IT THROUGH

⧗ In what ways have you felt God's Holy Spirit working in your life?

⧗ St Paul talks about the fruit of the Spirit (Galatians 5.22–23) – they are the qualities of character which the Holy Spirit creates in a person. Share with each other any time when you have been feeling bad about somebody and have asked God to give you the power to love them. What happened?

⧗ Have any of you experienced anything which you would consider miraculous – the result of God's supernatural power at work?

⧗ Have you heard of the Charismatic Movement in the church? If not, ask your parish priest to explain what it is.

# Christian beliefs about the Holy Spirit

● **The Holy Spirit is the third person of the Trinity.** God expresses himself in three forms: Father, Son and Holy Spirit. God the Father creates and sustains the world. Jesus the Son was God in human form showing us what God is like. God the Holy Spirit is God in action in our world.

● **We speak of the Holy Spirit as God with us now.** The Holy Spirit is not just a force or influence – the Holy Spirit is a person. The Spirit, the power of God at work, was seen throughout Jesus' ministry: at his baptism the Spirit appeared as a dove; the Spirit drove Jesus into the wilderness to be tempted by the Devil; it was by the power of the Spirit that Jesus performed his miracles and taught – the people listening to Jesus recognized that he spoke as one with special authority and power. Jesus told his disciples that when he had gone from them God the Father would send them 'The Helper, the Holy Spirit [who] will teach you everything and make you remember all that I have told you' (John 14.26). After his death and resurrection all the believers were gathered together when the Holy Spirit came upon them in power. The account can be found in Acts 2. The Church celebrates this event today at Pentecost (also called Whit Sunday).

● **The Holy Spirit is the life-giving Spirit.** The word used for Spirit in the Bible (*pneuma, ruach*) can mean 'breath' or 'wind'. The Holy Spirit is the one who gives life. Therefore in the story of the creation of the world God gave Adam the breath of life and he became a living being. Without breath there would be no life. Throughout the Bible the Holy Spirit is shown actively at work in people to give them new life, God's life.

● **The Holy Spirit is at work in human beings.** The New Testament talks of the Holy Spirit as God personally at work in the lives of believers. The Christian life is life lived in the power of the Holy Spirit. Like breath and wind the Holy Spirit is invisible – he is known through what he does. Traditionally the Church has spoken of the sevenfold gifts of the Holy Spirit

## . . . more Christian beliefs about the Holy Spirit

at work in people. These can be traced to Isaiah 11.1–3. They are:

**Wisdom** – to see things as God sees them.

**Understanding** – of God's revelation to us.

**Counsel** – to help us to see what we should do in difficult situations.

**Inward Strength** – to do God's will.

**Knowledge** – of the truth.

**True Godliness** – to feel that we are in a loving relationship with God and are brothers and sisters to all people.

**Fear of the Lord** – to give us an earnestness to do what God wishes.

At confirmation the Bishop prays a special prayer over the candidates, asking the Spirit to supply them with all seven of these gifts to help them in their Christian life.

- The Holy Spirit is shown working in the lives of believers in a number of ways:

  – **The Holy Spirit lives in believers, making a home in their hearts** (Ephesians 3.16–17), guiding them (Romans 8.9–11). The Spirit helps people to pray: 'the Spirit comes to help us, weak as we are. For we do not know how we ought to pray; the Spirit himself pleads with God for us' (Romans 8.26).

  – **The Spirit lives in people helping us to become more like Jesus.** The Holy Spirit gives people power to live as Christians. He has been called the 'go-between God' because he goes between Jesus and us. The Holy Spirit works in people to transform their characters to become more like Jesus. The qualities which the Spirit develops in people are known as the fruit of the Holy Spirit: 'the Spirit produces love, joy, peace, patience, kindness, goodness, faithfulness, humility and self control' (Galatians 5.22–23). This process of changing into the likeness of Jesus is called 'sanctification' (to be made holy). Paul summarizes the gradual process of sanctification in this way: 'We are being changed into his likeness from one

degree of glory to another. This comes from the Lord who is Spirit.' Christians experience this change as a battle between the new person the Spirit is creating and the old sinful person.

- **The Holy Spirit helps people to understand what God has revealed in the Bible.** Christians ask God to speak to them through the words of the Bible. It is the Holy Spirit which reveals to them the meaning of God's words. Without the Holy Spirit the words of the Bible can sound dull and meaningless, but he opens our hearts and ears to hear God speaking to us through the words of the Bible.

- Jesus told his disciples to carry on his work. **The Holy Spirit distributes among Christians a variety of spiritual gifts in order to do this.** No believer is without a gift. Different kinds of special gifts are named in 1 Corinthians 12.4–11. They are: service, wisdom, knowledge, healing, preaching, discernment, speaking in tongues. The Charismatic Movement has made people more aware of these spiritual gifts.

- To be filled with the Holy Spirit is never a once-and-for-all experience. **Christians are to ask continually for God to give them his Holy Spirit.** Sometimes the Holy Spirit will come in memorable ways, like on the day of Pentecost. But not all comings are like that. Sometimes the Holy Spirit works in quieter ways – to make our faith stronger, to give us courage, to guide us, etc.

● The Spirit is the power of God at work in the sacraments, for example:

– **At Baptism:** The making of new Christians is the work of the Holy Spirit in us.  As Jesus put it: 'Unless a man is born again of water and the Spirit, he cannot see or enter the Kingdom of God.' Jesus talked about the Holy Spirit as 'living water' (John 7.37–39). Water is a symbol of life as well as a cleansing agent. Both these images are important ways of speaking of what the Holy Spirit does at baptism.

– At the centre of the **Eucharist** there is a prayer to the Holy Spirit: 'Grant that by the power of the Holy Spirit, these gifts of bread and wine may be to us his body and blood.' God's power is at work in the form of the Holy Spirit to make Jesus present in the bread and wine, and present in our lives.

## BIBLE STUDY

Before his death Jesus told his disciples that it would be necessary for him to go away in order that the Holy Spirit might come to be their helper (John 15.26; 16.7). On the fiftieth day after Easter, at Pentecost, Jesus' followers were all gathered in Jerusalem. Suddenly the power of the Holy Spirit came upon them. Read the account in Acts 2.1–4.

◆ What did the multitude of people see and hear? Although you cannot see wind you can see the results of its power. Similarly you can see the power of the Holy Spirit in people's lives, changing them. Like fire the Holy Spirit burns away things which are wrong, and makes people's lives beautiful. Fire is the symbol of God's presence.

◆ In what ways were the apostles changed people when they received the power of the Holy Spirit in their lives? Think about how they had reacted when Jesus was arrested and crucified and how after the giving of the Holy Spirit they started to spread the gospel.

## FOR PRAYER & REFLECTION

*God, who from of old*
*taught the hearts of your faithful people*
*by sending to them the light of your Holy Spirit:*
*grant us by the same Spirit*
*to have a right judgement in all things,*
*and evermore to rejoice in his holy comfort;*
*through the merits of Christ Jesus our Saviour,*
*who is alive and reigns with you,*
*in the unity of the Holy Spirit,*
*one God, now and for ever.*

## SOME PRAYER TOPICS . . .

Ask the Holy Spirit to enter into your life to:

❖ help you to become more like Jesus
❖ change habits and attitudes
❖ help you understand the Bible.

# *T*HE CHURCH

*The Anglican Church maintains the historic threefold ministry of bishops, priests and deacons. Its ministers are ordained by bishops according to authorized forms of service, with prayer and the laying on of hands.*

## A worldwide community

Imagine the landscape of any town or village in Great Britain, North or South America and many parts of Africa, Australia, New Zealand or Europe without a church. Almost every community of any size has a church. Many of these are the oldest building in their community.

For generations, the followers of Jesus have needed somewhere to meet and worship. This remains the same today. Some people may go to church only occasionally but we still need large spaces in which to gather for weddings, funerals, baptisms and festivals.

Wherever 'the Church' has met its members have needed a special building, a church. But the Church is first and foremost not a building. It is we ourselves, the people who belong to Christ.

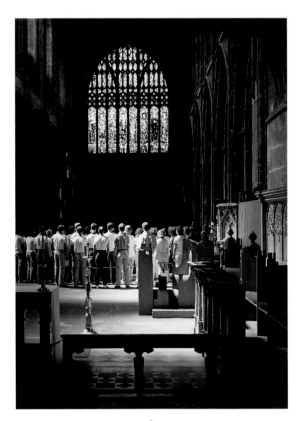

*Young people use the ancient space at Chester Cathedral for modern worship. Churches are constantly adapted to meet contemporary needs.*

## The Body of Christ

Jesus taught that he came to save sinners. The result of this was that the Christian Church from its very beginning has welcomed people regardless of their religious, ethnic or social status. This was following Jesus' example of accepting those whom the rest of society rejected. The most famous declaration of the openness of the Church can be found in St Paul's letter to the Christians in Galatia:

*All of you who were baptized into Christ have clothed yourselves with Christ. There is neither Jew nor Greek, slave nor free, male nor female, for you are all one in Christ Jesus. (Galatians 3.27–28)*

St Paul believed that baptism included a Christian in 'The Body of Christ'. As limbs and organs each have their part in the body, so do individual Christians within the life of the Church. Paul writes: 'The body is a unit, though it is made up of many parts; and though all its parts are many, they form one body. So it is with Christ' (1 Corinthians 12.12).

## The People of God

'The People of God' is another name for the Church. The first letter of Peter to the Churches of Asia Minor describes them as

*a chosen people, a royal priesthood, a holy nation, a people belonging to God, that you may declare the praises of him who called you out of darkness into his wonderful light. (1 Peter 2.9)*

Membership of this people is open to all those who respond to God's call to discipleship. This includes the poor and outcast. This means that the Church today has to be open to everyone and avoid showing racial or social prejudice.

# One, holy, catholic and apostolic

Anglicans proclaim that they are part of 'One, holy, catholic and apostolic Church'.

*One:* Although the 'visible' Church (i.e. the Church as an institution) is divided, all Christians believe in one God and the one Lord Jesus Christ; and almost all churches nowadays recognize one another's baptism. In Christ we are all members of the one Christian Church, even though it is divided into different 'structures' in the world.

*Holy:* We tend to use this word to mean especially good, but its Old Testament meaning includes a sense of someone or something being set aside or dedicated to God. To call the Church 'holy' means that it is dedicated to God.

# Christian beliefs about the Church

- **The Christian Church has its origins in the group of disciples whom Jesus gathered around him** at the beginning of his ministry.

- They deserted him at his arrest and crucifixion but **they regrouped to be the first witnesses of his resurrection and to continue his work** once he had ascended into heaven.

- **They formed the first Church** (in Greek *ecclesia* meaning 'those called together') **in Jerusalem**. They were **equipped for their work by the gift of the Spirit at Pentecost**.

- **This early Church lived a very simple life** and continued to preach the gospel and heal people as Jesus had done. Through the work of St Peter and St Paul in particular, offshoots of this Church were planted all over the Roman Empire.

- There were early Christian communities all over the known world, and from the beginning they kept in touch with each other and believed that the Holy Spirit bound them together. As the apostles died out they handed authority to bishops, to continue their leadership in the churches they had founded.

- **The bishops were an important sign of this unity.** They were a focus for the churches in their oversight (which formed a 'see', i.e. 'something overseen', or 'diocese') and the bishops were also linked to each other. This link was expressed by their common defence of the truth of the Christian Faith. By handing on authority through the ordination of bishops in every generation a link was also maintained with the original apostolic faith.

- **Bishops were assisted by deacons , and by priests who ran parishes for them.**

- Unfortunately, **this unity of Christians has been disrupted many times in the past 2,000 years**, most notably in 1054, when East and West divided, and in the sixteenth century when the Reformation occurred.

➔ *page 35*

We shouldn't, therefore, expect the Church to be a community of people who are unfailingly good but a community of people trying to be good, dependent upon God's help and forgiveness. The first letter of John reminds us of this:

> If we claim to be without sin, we deceive ourselves and the truth is not in us. If we confess our sins, he is faithful and just and will forgive us our sins and purify us from all unrighteousness. (1 John 1.8–9)

If we dedicate ourselves to God, he will help us to change.

**Catholic:** This is a word with many different meanings. People often use it to mean Roman Catholic. But its underlying meaning is 'universal'.

Christians believe that Christ is present in a full or 'whole' way wherever people pray or are gathered to worship him.

It can also have the additional meaning of 'possessing the whole faith'. Anglicans believe that they have faithfully received and handed on the faith of the Apostles.

**Apostolic:** This reminds us that the faith which we believe comes ultimately from the apostles and has been handed down faithfully since that time. Belief in Christ is rooted in historical events and the trustworthy public transmission of witness to them.

# Bishops, priests and deacons

The service of baptism reminds us that all Christians belong to a 'royal priesthood' called to serve Christ and our 'neighbour'. However, in the Churches that have bishops (e.g. Roman Catholic, Orthodox and Anglican), some Christians are called to serve in the three 'orders' of ministry, bishops, priests and deacons, whose roots can be detected in 1 Timothy, Acts and elsewhere in the New Testament. Each order has a particular role to fulfil on behalf of the whole Church.

- **bishops** – to oversee the Church, to have responsibility for protecting the Gospel from being taught wrongly and, particularly, to be a focus of the unity of the Church's life. This is why they are responsible for the ordination of new bishops, priests and deacons and preside at the Eucharist when they are present.

- **priests** – to celebrate the Church's sacraments (apart from confirmation and ordination). Through the sacraments they mediate (provide a channel for) the salvation which Jesus brings to us. However, they would not be able to do this without the work done by deacons or the work that they themselves undertake which a deacon might also perform. It is important to realize that ordination to the priesthood does not make someone cease to be a deacon.

- **deacons** – to look after people's welfare, for example, through visiting the sick and lonely, but also through making the whole Church aware of their needs. Just as Jesus had to be born on earth and live among people before he could bring them to salvation, so the deacon's work is to make Christ present in the community (to 'incarnate' him). In such a way, the deacon prepares the ground for the priest's work of celebrating the sacraments, through which Christ's salvation is brought to us. In worship, the deacon also has the distinctive roles of reading the Gospel and collecting together the people's intercessions (prayers) for common use. Deacons provide the foundation for the work of both priests and bishops.

## THINKING IT THROUGH

⧗ What is 'The Anglican Communion'?

⧗ How would you respond to someone who said 'I can be a Christian without going to Church'?

### . . . more Christian beliefs about the Church

● **The Anglican Church** began when the Church of England removed itself from the Pope's authority at the Reformation, but kept the historic ministry of bishops, priests and deacons in unbroken succession. British colonies had their own offshoots of the Church of England, which eventually became independent Anglican provinces. **This family of Churches is known as the Anglican Communion** and has about 60 million Anglicans worldwide. The Archbishop of Canterbury is titular head of all the bishops in the Anglican Communion, who meet together at the Lambeth Conference every ten years.

● **Lay people (those not ordained) play an increasing role in the life and work of the Churches of the Anglican Communion today.** For example, the Church of England has a General Synod (a kind of parliament for the Church) which has Houses of Bishops, Clergy and Laity. Beneath this national structure are diocesan and deanery synods and parish councils. It is important to remember that all Christians, not just clergy, have a vocation – that is, a calling to some special ministry or service for Christ in his Church.

● **Since the Second World War, in particular, the different denominations have made great efforts to recover their unity (the movement is called *ecumenism*).** There are many local ecumenical projects, where Christians of different denominations work and worship together to a considerable degree.

● The mass media and the experience of having those who believe in other faiths as our neighbours have also made **Christians increasingly aware of the need for dialogue with other faiths.**

## BIBLE STUDY

Acts 2.41–47

This gives us a description of life in the first Christian Church to be formed after Jesus' resurrection and ascension. Its simplicity of life has provided an ideal to countless generations of Christians since.

◆ What were the main features of life in the earliest Christian Church described in this passage?

◆ Does it differ from the Church as you know it?

◆ What changes should we seek in the life of the Church to which we belong?

## FOR PRAYER & REFLECTION

*O God of unchangeable power and eternal light, look favourably on thy whole Church, that wonderful and sacred mystery; and by the tranquil operation of thy perpetual providence carry out the work of man's salvation; and let the whole world feel and see that things which were cast down are being raised up; that those which had grown old are being made new; and that all things are returning into unity through him by whom all things were made, even thy Son Jesus Christ our Lord.*
(Gelasian Sacramentary, fifth century, from *The Book of Christian Prayer*)

### SOME PRAYER TOPICS . . .

❖ For the life of our parish.

❖ For particular people in the parish who need our prayers.

❖ For our bishop and other parishes in the diocese.

❖ For Christians throughout the world, especially those who find it difficult to meet and worship.

# $T$HE CREEDS

*The Anglican Church is part of the one, holy, catholic, and apostolic Church, worshipping the one true God, Father, Son, and Holy Spirit. It professes the faith uniquely revealed in the holy Scriptures and set forth in the catholic creeds. (From the service for the ordination of a bishop)*

When you pick up a newspaper, you read the headlines and the summary at the beginning of an article first. The same happens when you go to the theatre. You'll find an introduction to the play in the programme. And books have a blurb on the back to tell you what's inside.

The creeds of the Christian Church are a bit like this. They are phrased in more formal language but they provide a kind of 'outside cover' for the Christian faith. They give you an idea of what you're going to get when you read on and know more.

They are used in church at many services and provide a summary of what the faith is about.

*The Nicene Creed proclaims the Christian faith and lists the beliefs upon which life should be based. It is a call to action.*

(Dom Antony Sutch,
    Headmaster of Downside School)

The two most widely used creeds are the Apostles' Creed and the Nicene Creed.

## The Apostles' Creed

*I believe in God, the Father almighty,
creator of heaven and earth.*

*I believe in Jesus Christ, his only Son, our Lord,
who was conceived by the Holy Spirit,
born of the Virgin Mary,
suffered under Pontius Pilate,
was crucified, died, and was buried;
he descended to the dead.
On the third day he rose again;
he ascended into heaven,
he is seated at the right hand of the Father,
and he will come to judge the living and the dead.
I believe in the Holy Spirit,
the holy catholic Church,
the communion of saints,
the forgiveness of sins,
the resurrection of the body,
and the life everlasting.*
                *Amen.*

God is the Creator of the World and Jesus' relationship to him is spelt out: he is God's 'only Son', 'born of the Virgin Mary'. He is unique. Then the great acts of his life are outlined: he suffered, died and was buried at a particular time in history (which we know from the reference to Pontius Pilate). He was raised from the dead, ascended into heaven and will come again as a judge. This is echoed in the acclamation in the Eucharist: 'Christ has died, Christ is risen, Christ will come again'.

# Christian beliefs about the creeds

*A creed has come to be recognized as a concise, formal, universally accepted and authorized statement of the main points of Christian faith. (Alister McGrath, Christian Theology – An Introduction)*

- **Creeds are summaries of Christian belief** which developed from the questions asked by bishops at baptism. However, it is important to realize that they also play the role of a standard or coat of arms. We are meant to rally to them just as soldiers did to a familiar flag in a battle.

- **There are traces of very short creeds in the New Testament.** At the end of his first letter to the Christians at Corinth, St Paul writes: 'For what I received I passed on to you as of first importance: that Christ died for our sins according to the Scriptures, that he was buried, that he was raised on the third day according to the Scriptures, and that he appeared to Peter, and then to the Twelve.' (I Corinthians 15.3, 4)

- **Christians also often produced creeds when they were persecuted.** A summary of belief could be used to counter accusations.

- **The most famous creeds date from the fourth and fifth centuries**, when there were violent disagreements between Christians, especially about the nature of Jesus.

- **The Nicene Creed** takes its name from the Council of Nicaea (AD 325), where the question 'In what way was Jesus God and Man' was debated. Arguments about the definition of true belief had become very important as Christianity had been the religion of the Roman Empire since AD 313. The Apostles' Creed was first known in its present form in about AD 400.

- **The Apostles' Creed** is used at baptism and the Nicene Creed at the Eucharist.

- Confirmation courses (like this one) are often closely linked to the different parts of the creeds, just as preparation for baptism was in the ancient Church. In those days, though, preparation for baptism could sometimes take three years as it was thought to be such an important step to take.

- The creeds are public summaries of faith accepted by Christians everywhere, virtually regardless of denomination (branch of the Church, e.g., Anglican, Roman Catholic, Baptist, Orthodox).

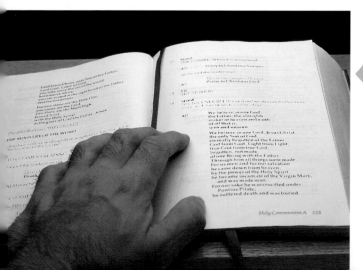

*The Nicene Creed is frequently said at the Eucharist. The Apostles' Creed is probably the best known form of the creed in the West. It concentrates on the work of the Trinity, i.e. God as Father, Son and Holy Spirit, giving greatest attention to Jesus.*

# The Nicene Creed

*We believe in one God,*
*the Father, the Almighty,*
*maker of heaven and earth,*
*of all that is,*
*seen and unseen.*

*We believe in one Lord, Jesus Christ,*
*the only Son of God,*
*eternally begotten of the Father,*
*God from God, Light from Light,*
*true God from true God,*
*begotten, not made,*
*of one Being with the Father.*
*Through him all things were made.*
*For us men and for our salvation*
*he came down from heaven:*
*by the power of the Holy Spirit*
*he became incarnate of the Virgin Mary, and was made man.*

*For our sake he was crucified under Pontius Pilate;*
*he suffered death and was buried.*
*On the third day he rose again*
*in accordance with the Scriptures;*
*he ascended into heaven*
*and is seated at the right hand of the Father.*
*He will come again in glory*
*to judge the living and the dead,*
*and his kingdom will have no end.*

*We believe in the Holy Spirit,*
*the Lord, the giver of life,*
*who proceeds from the Father and the Son.*
*With the Father and the Son he is worshipped and glorified.*
*He has spoken through the Prophets.*
*We believe in one holy catholic and apostolic Church.*
*We acknowledge one baptism for the forgiveness of sins.*
*We look for the resurrection of the dead,*
*and the life of the world to come. Amen.*

**In this detail from Paolo Uccello's 'Battle of San Romano', the commander's banner provides a rallying point for the troops.**

The Nicene Creed is longer than but very similar to the Apostles' Creed. It differs in the detail it gives about the role of Jesus in creation ('Through him all things were made') and salvation ('For our sake he was crucified'). It also emphasizes the bond between Father, Son and Holy Spirit: Jesus 'is seated at the right hand of the Father' and the Holy Spirit 'proceeds from the Father and the Son'.

Much of the language may seem rather technical but its main purpose is to stress that Jesus was truly God and man (see Chapter 2, 'Human Nature & Sin', and Chapter 3, 'Jesus: Life & Ministry').

## THINKING IT THROUGH

⧗ Summarize your own most important beliefs, making them into a creed.

⧗ How can 'knowing what you believe' alter your life?

⧗ Do you think that learning the Creed by heart could be helpful?

## BIBLE STUDY

**1 Corinthians 15.1–11**

St Paul explains how the gospel has been passed on to him and how he now passes it on to others. He is the most unusual person to be doing this as he had persecuted Christians. But the 'grace of God' has made him what he is.

◆ How satisfactory is it to summarize the gospel as briefly as St Paul?

◆ Why do you think he mentions that the resurrection (and the teaching in general) is a matter of public knowledge?

◆ What does this passage teach about the power of God in an individual life?

*The creeds, which are said at many church services, are like a banner to accompany us on our pilgrimage through life.*

## FOR PRAYER & REFLECTION

*Almighty and everlasting God,*
*increase in us your gift of faith*
*that, forsaking what lies behind*
*and reaching out to that which is before,*
*we may run the way of your commandments*
*and win the crown of everlasting joy;*
*through Jesus Christ your Son our Lord,*
*who is alive and reigns with you,*
*in the unity of the Holy Spirit,*
*one God, now and for ever.*

## SOME PRAYER TOPICS . . .

❖ For a greater understanding of Christian belief.

❖ To experience faith as something personal.

❖ To live the beliefs of the Creed.

❖ For courage to stand up for what we believe.

❖ For God's help for those who are persecuted for their beliefs.

# $T$HE BIBLE

*Blessed Lord, who caused all holy
scriptures to be written for our learning,
help us . . . to hear them, to read,
mark, learn and inwardly digest them.*

## A dangerous book

It is December 1991 and a party of
young people from British schools are
visiting the Soviet Union for the first
time. It is a time of great political
change. Everyone is talking about a new
people's revolution in favour of
Western-style democracy.

But conditions are still difficult. There
are food shortages and most of the
young people have brought food with
them to give away.

There is a long wait at the baggage
carousel. Out of sight, some of the
baggage is being interfered with by the
handlers, probably searching for food

**The Bible has always
had the power to
liberate people,
especially the poor
and oppressed. Here
it is being used in a
Bible study meeting
in a Mexican 'base
community'.**

and valuables. Two cases are declared
lost. The rest of the party, now reunited
with their luggage, face the last hurdle
of customs while their teachers protest
about the lost luggage.

Suddenly, there is a commotion. A tall,
thin man in his thirties is involved in a
heated argument with a customs official
who has found Bibles in his suitcase.
Police quickly arrive and he is arrested.
This is astonishing to the Western
onlookers. Bibles are something given as
baptism presents or handed out for
lessons in school. No one could get
arrested for having a Bible at home.

## Why can the Bible
be dangerous?

The Bible is dangerous because it has
the power to change lives. It has
changed more lives than any other
book. At its worst, disagreements over
its meaning have been among the
causes of wars of religion. At its best, it
has inspired self-sacrifice, given
meaning to many people's lives, led
scholars to devote a lifetime to its study,
and provided the raw material for
innumerable works of art.

For example, at an open-air Christian
meeting in Chile, when a member of the
audience heard the good news about
Jesus, he approached the speaker. To
show his desire to change his way of life,

he handed over a suitcase containing a machine gun and a bomb.

A simple sign of its continued importance can be seen in our law courts. When a trial is held and Christian witnesses have to swear to tell the truth, they are first asked to do this on the Holy Bible. This is because Christians see the Bible as the source of the most important truths about life and to swear on it should guarantee that they tell the truth in their evidence.

*Love of the Bible has inspired scholars and artists, as we can see in this elaborate illustration at the beginning of St Matthew's Gospel in the Lindisfarne Gospels.*

*The Bible isn't a history book or a poetry book or a cookbook, even though there are elements of all these things in it. Essentially it is a faith book . . . It is the story of a God who believed in his people, the Israelites, and how they learnt to believe in him, discovering him as their lives and adventures unfolded. In its pages you can always see the people's faith, or lack of it, even though you can't see their God. And if you are looking for him, mostly you can see footprints, marks in the sand, saying God was here. (Tony Robinson, Heart and Soul, BBC1)*

# Christian beliefs about the Bible

- Christians believe **that Jesus is the Word of God** (see John 1.1–18) **and that the Bible is the primary witness to his life and saving work.** Without it, we would have no reliable information about God's purpose in history or about his Son, Jesus Christ.

- The **books of the Bible were written and collected by people who responded to God's Word** and recorded it for the benefit of those who came after them.

- **The Bible tells the story of how God has spoken and acted in history.** It begins with stories of creation which teach that the world, its creatures and human beings are not an accident but willed by God. Human frailty, though, has spoiled the world and led God to restore it. This is the story of the Israelites from Abraham to the coming of Jesus.

- **God called Abraham and his descendants to a special relationship with him.** When they were in captivity in Egypt, he rescued them for life in the Promised Land, which they reached after their faith had been tested by wandering for 40 years in the wilderness of the Sinai Desert. Once established in the Promised Land (modern Israel), they went through many ups and downs in their service of God.

- The prophets spoke out against them when they strayed from doing God's will and warned them that they would return to captivity if they did not repent.

- In 586 BC, they were driven into exile in Babylon, which led them to question whether God had failed them. The answer given by the prophet Isaiah was that they had failed God. But this did not mean that God would abandon them. If they returned to him, they would be able to rebuild Jerusalem. Connected with this hope was the expectation that a special person, a Messiah, would come to redeem Israel.

➔ *page 42*

## . . . more Christian beliefs about the Bible

- **The major theme of the Old Testament is that God calls his people and though they stray he never gives up on them,** answering their prayers even in the worst of times.

- **God eventually became man to save them,** which is the 'good news' (gospel) which the New Testament records.

- This man, Jesus, was rejected by his own people and died a criminal's death. But he was raised from the dead. **Jesus' resurrection is the climax of God's work of bringing salvation to humanity.**

- **The importance of this story comes from the fact that it is historical.** The resurrection is not a science fiction story about a hero whose exploits we enjoy watching on television, nor is it just an interesting idea. As St Paul says, ' . . . if Christ has not been raised from death, then we have nothing to preach and you have nothing to believe' (1 Corinthians 15.14). For this reason, Christians need to be able to trust the historical evidence in the Bible.

- **However, the Bible contains interpretation as well as history.** For example, it does not simply tell us about the wanderings of a little-known people in the Sinai desert. It also tells us that they were a chosen people and that this was a testing time required by God. In other words, the bare facts are given a context and a meaning.

- We do this all the time when we report something. For example, when the late Mr Rabin (the Prime Minister of Israel) and Mr Arafat (the Palestinian leader) met each other on the White House lawn in the presence of President Clinton in September 1994, we needed to know that they had been mortal enemies for over 40 years to see the significance of their shaking hands. Otherwise, it would only have been the unremarkable event of two elderly men greeting each other in a garden.

→ page 43

# How to use the Bible in our lives

The Bible is a living book. Christians have always turned to it to understand what God expects of them.

Just opening it and beginning to read can have a remarkable effect, as Olympic athlete Kriss Akabusi found:

> I went to the Commonwealth Games in 1986 in a bit of a turmoil, wondering what life was about. As I went into the room there was a Good News Bible on my bed. I picked it up and started reading it. I met a character there I'd never met before, and Jesus Christ challenged me to think about what the real meaning of life was. And I liked the things he had to say. Most importantly he seemed to respect me for who I was as a person, and I was challenged. Nine months later I asked him to make himself more real to me, and my faith grew from there.

This story shows that there is nothing 'out of touch' about the main stories of the gospels. They describe many situations, such as when people are sick or suffer, in which it is easy for us to imagine ourselves.

It is important and enjoyable to study the Bible with others. Just as we learn another language best by spending time with people who speak it, so we will learn the language of the Bible best by becoming part of the community of the Church where it is a living language. In the life of the Church, the Bible has been a 'living language' for almost 2,000 years.

To make connections between the Bible and the present, many Christians study particular passages of the Bible either on their own or as members of a Bible study group.

## Where to start

The gospels of Matthew and Luke are probably the best parts of the Bible to begin with as they contain many familiar stories.

It is not a good idea to try to read the Bible from the beginning and work through, as some of the books you will come across very early, like Leviticus, are very technical.

You could use the *Revised Common Lectionary*, which provides readings for every Sunday over a cycle of three

years. You simply have to find where you are in the cycle and start from there.

It is useful to have a commentary (a book written by a biblical scholar which helps you to understand what the Bible means) or a set of reader's notes, which are briefer than a commentary.

## What to do

● Read a passage. Keep what you choose simple and brief.

● Read a commentary. Discuss it with others (if they are in a group).

● Pray about it.

*It is the call in these days of busy-ness, frenzy and rush to stop, to look and to listen, to have the courage to carve out a 'quiet time'.* (David Hope, Archbishop of York)

Throughout this book, we have suggested passages at the end of each chapter for you to do this for yourselves.

By studying the Bible in this way, you will be putting it at the heart of your life as a Christian.

● In the same way, if we did not know the context of Jesus' story, all we would know would be this: 'Once, there was an idealistic young man who taught the crowds who would listen to him, healed sick people, and ran into trouble with the authorities. After an illegal, secret trial, he underwent a public execution.' Instead, we know that his disciples sensed a unique presence of God in him and that he appeared to them raised from the dead three days after they had fled fearing for their own lives.

● **The full interpretation of the facts took years to develop.** In the different books of the New Testament, we can gradually see the way in which the first Christians came to terms with the facts of Jesus' life. So, from his letters, we may read about the way in which Paul, who had persecuted Jesus, came to believe the gospel and teach the church at Corinth that 'God was making mankind his friends through Christ. God did not keep an account of their sins' (2 Corinthians 5.19).

## The books themselves

The contents of the New and Old Testaments of the Bible which we know today took over a century after Jesus' lifetime to be agreed upon. Those books which all Christians accept are said to be 'canonical' (from a Greek word for 'measure'). They alone measure up to universal standards of historical accuracy and importance.

There has always been some disagreement about another group of books, usually called the Apocrypha (literally meaning 'hidden'). They date from the later period of the Old Testament – that is, the time just before Jesus, and are usually printed in Bibles between the Old Testament and the New. They are like books in the back room of a library, which are taken out occasionally but not continuously referred to. They have been influential in Christian history but do not have the same status as the canonical Old and New Testaments.

## The Old Testament

The Old Testament, which was written in Hebrew, tells the story of God's dealings with the Jewish people before the time of Jesus. It is the story of how God made a covenant (a promise) with them, but how they kept breaking their side of the promise. However, in spite of this, God continued to love them and call them back to him.

The books of the Old Testament, which were originally written in Hebrew, are important because Jesus and the early Christians treated them as having lasting value. In fact, the early Christians had no other Bible but the Jewish one. Also, the point of what Jesus achieved would be lost if we did not have a trustworthy record of what God had done beforehand and the way in which human beings had strayed away from God.

The history of the development of the Old Testament is complicated but, basically, the books which passed into it are associated with key figures in Jewish history, like Moses (Exodus), David and Solomon (1 and 2 Samuel; 1 and 2 Kings; 1 and 2 Chronicles) and the prophets (who often have their own books, e.g. Hosea).

The Old Testament was the Bible of Jesus and his followers. The gospels and letters written after Jesus' death and resurrection all assumed familiarity with the Old Testament. This means that we need to know the Old Testament if we are to understand the New Testament. How much this is so is apparent once you use a Bible with footnotes on each page. Notice how many references there are to the books of the Old Testament.

## The New Testament

There is now no disagreement among Christians about which books should be included in the New Testament. However, for the first few centuries, there was hesitation over certain books, particularly Hebrews, which is anonymous, James, 2 Peter, 2 and 3 John, Jude and Revelation.

The main information about the life of Jesus is found in the four gospels, Matthew, Mark, Luke and John. The Acts of the Apostles tell the story of the spread of the gospel and the founding of the first Christian communities. The Letters reveal more about their life and the efforts of their leaders, especially St Paul, to apply the gospel to everyday life. The Book of Revelation uses vivid language to describe a vision of the end of time.

# The Bible in prayer and church services

When you go to church services, you will often hear psalms from the Old Testament sung just as they are written there or adapted into hymns or choruses.

Usually, passages from the Old and New Testaments will be read to the congregation and explained in sermons.

In the Eucharist, the central prayer recalling the Lord's Supper is taken virtually unchanged from the New Testament. Many of the formal prayers used are based on quotations from the Bible.

## THINKING IT THROUGH

⏳ Why can the Bible be seen as a dangerous book?

⏳ Why does it matter so much to Christians?

⏳ Why do Christians trust the Bible?

⏳ Choose a passage from the Bible that is important for you. Explain to the other members of your group why you value it.

## FOR PRAYER & REFLECTION

*Blessed Lord,*

*who caused all holy scriptures to be written for our learning:*

*help us so to hear them,*

*to read, mark, learn and inwardly digest them,*

*that, through patience, and the comfort of your holy word,*

*we may embrace and for ever hold fast the hope of everlasting life,*

*which you have given us in our Saviour Jesus Christ.*

## BIBLE STUDY

Read the parable of the Vineyard (Mark 12.1–11) which summarizes the whole outline of God's involvement with humanity.

In this story the owner is God, the people of Israel the first tenants, the servants his prophets, the son Jesus and the people to whom the vineyard is ultimately given, the Gentiles (non-Jews).

* What does this story teach us about God's nature?

* How could this story be seen as warning people about being complacent about having God's favour?

* In what ways do you feel that we can be like the tenants who were reluctant to pay their rent?

## SOME PRAYER TOPICS . . .

❖ Hearing God's word through the Scriptures.

❖ Asking for God's help in understanding the Bible.

❖ To hear God's Word for me through the reading of the Bible.

❖ For help for those who find it difficult to obtain Bibles or are persecuted for owning them.

# *L*IVING AS A CHRISTIAN

*God, the giver of life,*
*whose Holy Spirit wells up within your*
*Church:*
*by the Spirit's gifts equip us to live the*
*gospel of Christ*
*     and make us eager to do your will.*

**Speaking out about Jesus has enabled many people today to get to know Christ.**

Changes in where we live and the people we live with affect the way we live. Simply moving from the town to the country, or changing schools, means that we have to adapt the way we behave. If you live in a small village, it's likely that everyone knows everyone else. Once you move to a town, you have to make more effort to get to know other people. Your first school may be small and everyone knows who you are. Your senior school will probably be bigger and you may well feel lost and wonder how to cope. Becoming a member of a church may equally shake up the way you behave.

Being a Christian should change the sort of person you are. Not in some holier-than-thou, goody-goody way. But Christians should be people who:

● are willing to talk about Jesus

● go out of their way to serve other people

● forgive others

● encourage those who are at odds to forgive one another.

In short, Christians are the companions and followers of Jesus and should live in a way which he would approve of. They are also mindful that the way they act now will affect the way in which they are judged in the life to come.

Innumerable books have been written about how to live as a Christian, but some ideas crop up in all of them.

Important ones are: conscience, forgiveness, judgement and a belief that God notices everything that we do.

# Conscience

Even small children rapidly develop a sense of right and wrong. As they grow older they usually become more sophisticated in their ability to reason about moral decisions. This capacity to reason about what is the right course of action is called *conscience*. We use the word conscience in a number of revealing ways. We talk about someone who takes care as being *conscientious*. People who have done something wrong have a *guilty conscience* and those who have behaved well will declare that they have a *clear conscience*.

Christians use their conscience properly when they consider the options available to them in the light of Scripture and tradition and through the guidance of the Spirit.

In practice, this means that we need to take part in a parish life where the Christian tradition is alive and where it is normal to discuss and pray about moral decisions.

# Repentance and forgiveness

*Then Peter came to Jesus and asked, 'Lord, if my brother keeps on sinning against me, how many times do I have to forgive him? Seven times?' 'No, not seven times,' answered Jesus, 'but seventy times seven.' (Matthew 18.21–22)*

Part of being human is that we all do things wrong and stand in need of forgiveness. Forgiveness is one of the most distinctive features of Christianity. Jesus himself forgave those who crucified him ('forgive them for they know not what they do'). He also taught about forgiveness in parables, the most famous of which was the parable of the Prodigal (Lost) Son (Luke 15.11–32). The younger of two sons asked his father for his inheritance. He went away to a far land and wasted it in loose living. Eventually, he had frittered it all away and was reduced to feeding pigs for a living, even eating their food. After a time, he thought that he could fare better if he returned home as a

servant in his father's house. By doing this, he repented. To his surprise, his father was looking out for him and embraced him with enthusiasm and ordered a celebratory meal to be prepared. In this story, the father represents God rejoicing at the repentance of a sinner.

Repentance literally means turning around or changing direction. It opens us to receiving forgiveness. Being forgiven helps us to rebuild our lives and start growing again. This isn't something which will happen only occasionally. We will find ourselves repenting and needing forgiveness over and

## Christian beliefs about how to live

● **There is no system of laws which Christians have to obey.** However, **there is the Great Commandment to love God and to love your neighbour as yourself.** This provides a framework within which all Christian teaching about moral decisions falls. The Ten Commandments also provide an essential framework, condemning killing, theft and adultery in particular.

● **Christians believe that the Holy Spirit has helped and continues to help us make moral decisions.** Consequently, Christians also refer to their tradition. However, we do not apply tradition unthinkingly. We reason and pray about how to apply it.

● Anglicans summarize this approach by saying that we **make decisions about what God wants by reference to Scripture, tradition and reason.** We first seek guidance from what the Bible teaches. Then we look to see how previous generations of Christians have interpreted that. All the time we are doing this, we are using that human faculty, reason, which distinguishes us from other creatures. It entails the prayerful use of our minds to discover what we should do with the help of the Spirit.

➔ *page 48*

- We are helped in this as individuals by the teaching of our bishops. Often when there is a difficult moral question, like divorce and re-marriage, the bishops study the question and publish guidelines, which Anglicans and especially priests who help their congregations can refer to when individuals are looking for moral guidance.

- Sometimes, such guidance comes from the bishops of all the Anglican churches worldwide (the Anglican Communion, which holds Lambeth Conferences every ten years to discuss the most important questions facing Anglicans). So, for example, the practice of artificial contraception has been thought permissible for Anglicans since the Lambeth Conference of 1930.

- Since Jesus particularly valued the poor and outcast and healed the sick, it is natural for Christians to feel special moral obligations towards those who are ill, poor or excluded from society.

- Christians will also campaign for political and social action. The involvement of the Anglican Church in South Africa in the effort to end apartheid is a good example of this.

**When there is great evil in society, as in South Africa under apartheid, speaking out about Jesus may make someone a 'prophet' and take the kind of courage shown by Archbishop Desmond Tutu.**

➔ *page 49*

over again.

*Being virtuous doesn't preclude slipping up and falling, once in a while. Being virtuous means getting up and trying again.* (Michel Quoist)

*Forgiveness humanises the forgiven. It does exactly the same to the forgiver.* (Dom Antony Sutch)

# Judgement

New Testament teaching about judgement provides a counterbalance to that about forgiveness.

A famous story (John 8) illustrates this. A woman had been caught committing adultery. Her accusers brought her before Jesus, expecting to exact the usual punishment of death by stoning. Jesus' response was to ask the person who had never sinned to cast the first stone. Since none could claim to be without sin, they all slipped away, the oldest, with the longest life in which to have sinned, being the first to go. Jesus is left facing the woman. He tells her to go away and sin no more.

The interesting point about this story is that Jesus does not treat her as if she had not sinned. Nor does he make her forgiveness depend upon her repentance. He simply warns her not to repeat her sin.

From this Christians recognize that God judges our wrong acts. But God also forgives us and expects us to be free to change our lives once we are forgiven.

# God sees everything

*I tell you, whenever you refused to help one of these least important ones, you refused to help me.* (Matthew 25.45)

The parable of the Sheep and the Goats (Matthew 25.31–46) gives a famous illustration of the way in which God notices all our good and evil acts and how important it is to respond to the needs of those who suffer.

Jesus describes a judgement which resembles the way in which a shepherd in the Holy Land separates sheep from goats (they are quite similar to the inexperienced eye). He judges as good all those who have fed the hungry, given refreshment to the thirsty, welcomed the stranger, clothed the needy, and visited the sick and those in prison. The bad are all those who have ignored these needs.

The remarkable feature of the story is that Jesus sees all these good acts as done to him and all the times when we have neglected to do them as a failure of love towards him.

This means that Christians should see Jesus as being at the heart of all of their moral decisions. In a way, we should ask ourselves this simple question when faced with a moral problem: *is this what I would do to Jesus?* Today some Christians wear bracelets with the letters WWJD. They stand for 'What would Jesus do?' This bracelet is a reminder that at all times we should act in the way Jesus would. We should *be* Jesus to others.

---

### ... *more Christian beliefs about how to live*

- A Christian society will be one where everyone is welcome regardless of social status or origins. As St Paul wrote, 'In Christ there is neither freeman nor slave, Jew nor Gentile' (1 Corinthians 12.13).

- One name for this community, united by belief and sharing of communion, is the Kingdom of God. One picture of this is of a banquet to which all are invited and where those who push for a better deal will be expected to give way to the humble.

- It is a community characterized by forgiveness. Jesus himself has time for the outcasts of his day, tax collectors, adulteresses and prostitutes. Since tax collectors made their living by collecting money for the hated Roman occupiers of Palestine and the penalty for adultery was death, his befriending of them was remarkable.

---

## Who is my neighbour?

The parable of the Sheep and the Goats should be coupled with that of the Good Samaritan (Luke 10.25–37). In the Sheep and Goats, anyone in need deserves our help. The parable of the Good Samaritan is making a similar point.

A lawyer asks Jesus, 'Who is my neighbour?' Jesus replies by telling the story of someone who is mugged and left for dead. Two 'worthies', a Levite and a priest, pass him by. Only a Samaritan, who belonged to a minority group looked down upon by Jesus' contemporaries, helped the injured man and arranged for him to be looked after. The lawyer, Jesus says, should 'Go, and do likewise.'

This implies that anyone we come across can be seen as our 'neighbour' and deserving of our help. Christians shouldn't be concerned only with their immediate families, friends and neighbours. Even strangers should be seen as neighbours. Such teaching underlies the Christian appeals for helping people abroad or those in our own society with whom we have no 'neighbourly' contact in the usual, narrow sense of the people whom we know.

# A change of character

We could sum up the whole of Christian moral teaching as a desire to have our character and attitude changed by God so that we are different in ourselves and in our behaviour towards others.

Whether I behave towards someone else as I would towards Jesus is less a matter of keeping to certain rules and more to do with a change of character. As the Holy Spirit works in the depth of our personalities, our whole way of seeing things and acting should change.

Our ancestors would have said that we should cultivate the seven great virtues: wisdom, fortitude, temperance, justice, faith, hope and love. We could draw up a simpler list to begin with. Christians should show honesty, thoughtfulness, sensitivity and compassion towards others. Or, to use other words, they should have integrity and exercise responsibility. In the Bible Peter provides a list of qualities which Christians should cultivate: goodness, knowledge, self-control, perseverance, godliness, brotherly kindness and love (2 Peter 1.5–7).

## BIBLE STUDY

Read Jesus' teaching about forgiveness in the Sermon on the Mount (Matthew 5.38–48).

Here Jesus is urging his followers to adopt an entirely different standard from those who would merely 'pay back' the harm done to them. He expects his disciples to show as much forgiveness and goodness as God.

- What attitude is represented by 'an eye for an eye'?
- Is Jesus' teaching too high an ideal?
- How might a Christian be helped in trying to practise this teaching?
- How do we expect Jesus to treat us if we fail to live up to his standard of forgiveness?

## FOR PRAYER & REFLECTION

St Francis composed this great prayer about peace and forgiveness.

*Lord, make us instruments of your peace.*
*Where there is hatred, let us sow love;*
*where there is injury, let there be pardon;*
*where there is discord, union;*
*where there is doubt, faith;*
*where there is despair, hope;*
*where there is darkness, light;*
*where there is sadness, joy;*
*for your mercy and for your truth's sake.*
*Amen.*

## SOME PRAYER TOPICS . . .

- Asking for God's forgiveness for those things which we regret doing.
- Help from God in understanding how to know and act upon God's will.
- Asking for help to be able to forgive others.
- Doing something to relieve the suffering of those whom we do not know personally.

## THINKING IT THROUGH

- If someone asked you to summarize what 'living as a Christian' meant, what would you say?
- How much should we be prepared to forgive others?
- Why should Christians be concerned for the welfare of others, even those whom they do not know?
- How do we practically discover what it is right to do?
- Should our Christian beliefs affect the way we vote?

# $P$RAYER & WORSHIP

## How do I pray?

A young man is dying of cancer. He is so weak that he can no longer climb the stairs and his family have made a bedroom downstairs for him. He has been asking his elder brother whether he is going to get better and his brother has broken the news to him that he is going to die.

A priest comes to visit and the young man asks him how to pray, as he has never really prayed very much and isn't sure how to go about it.

The priest says that it is like having a conversation. Just say to God what you feel. Tell him about your pain and tiredness, about your worries about your family and how they are going to cope after you've died. Tell God about all the things which you feel sorry about and regret as you look back over your life. Ask God for his help.

The young man seems to be happy with this but he asks again whether there are some special words which he can use. The priest suggests that they say the Lord's Prayer together. It is very moving to see the young man with great simplicity put his frail hands together and say the 'Our Father' in little more than a whisper. For the remaining days he is very calm and on the night before he dies, he is able to say goodbye to his whole family.

Most people are moved to prayer at the important moments of their lives. Confronted by illness, difficulties with marriage or friendships, major exams or other big problems, it seems natural to cry out to God. But we can also be moved to prayer by great beauty. Standing on top of a mountain on a clear day and contemplating the wonder of the created world, we feel awe at the majesty and beauty of the view.

In fact, on any occasion when we are lifted out of the ordinary, whether we feel pain or joy, we want to express it, not just to other people, but to God.

*Fundamental to prayer is a sense of awe at the beauty and scale of the world.*

The ways in which we do this are as varied as the ways in which we speak. We may pray to God speaking as simply as we would to members of our family. When we do this we are following Jesus' teaching that we should address God as 'Our Father'.

At other times, we may find set words a help. If we are feeling very emotional, set words may provide us with something solid to hold on to. Or they can help when we don't know what words to begin with.

Like other kinds of communication, prayer needs practice. We learn to speak, read and write by endless repetition and practice. Prayer becomes natural if we pray frequently and regularly.

Prayer, like conversation, is a two-way process. We need to listen to God as well as speak to him. Also, just as we sometimes have one-to-one conversations and at other times we are talking in the company of many others, so Christians also pray to God with other people. This is what happens in church services and in prayer groups.

> . . . most situations in life are like the soufflé or Yorkshire pud. It depends on how you take them whether they become delights or disasters, jokes or tragedies. That's why, when they happen, praying is so important. Practically speaking, prayer helps you like a cigarette – but without the nasty side-effects – because it allows you a pause. And in that pause is protection, because you have time to ask yourself what your problem is trying to tell you, what God is saying in it. Perhaps, there is a blessing wrapped up in there, if you stop panicking. (Rabbi Lionel Blue, *Bolts from the Blue*)

# Types of prayer

> I pray because I can't help myself. I pray because I'm helpless, I pray because the need flows out of me all the time, waking and sleeping. It doesn't change God, it changes me. (C. S. Lewis)

The main kinds of Christian prayer are: Adoration, Confession, Thanksgiving, and Supplication. They are often remembered by the abbreviation ACTS.

# Adoration – 'To be with God wondering'

As we look around at the world there is so much to praise God for. The world with its beauty and majesty can make you stand in awe and wonder. The view from a high mountain, the force of a great storm, the intricate beauty of plants, or the delicate mechanism of the human body, are all capable of stimulating a sense of awe. This can make us want to offer a prayer of adoration to God, the source of the 'awe-full' things. Sometimes, the sense of awe can be so great that we feel very small and humble, even terrified. Perhaps you feel this staring at a vast landscape from the top of a high mountain or from an aeroplane. This was the original sense of the word 'awful', which is often overused and loses its original force.

# Confession – 'To be with God ashamed'

Praying isn't always nice. When we do wrong we need to face up to what we have done and ask God to forgive us. As we know from the parable of the Lost (Prodigal) Son, and many other parts of Jesus' teaching, God wants to forgive everybody. But he also wants us to change (repent) and become more like him, which can be very hard.

# Thanksgiving –
## 'To be with God gratefully'

We all have so much to thank God for – our health, security, our family and friends. In offering God prayers of thanksgiving we are saying how grateful we are.

# Supplication –
## 'To be with God' with others in mind, 'that is intercession'

Jesus told his disciples, 'Ask, and you will receive; seek, and you will find' (Matthew 7.7). In prayer we should not just pray for our own needs but also for the needs of others. This is called intercession. By doing this we are not trying to twist God's arm to make him do things. We are joining with God in the spiritual battle he is waging against evil, against all that tries to destroy good. Intercessory prayer can be very demanding – it takes effort to put yourself into the position of another person, to think about what they may be feeling, feel their pain and offer it up to God to work in their situation. But our intercessory prayers for others must not take the place of action. God may well be asking us to do something about the situation. In this we need to seek God's guidance.

# Christian beliefs about prayer and worship

- Prayer can be defined as standing before God. In prayer we open our minds and hearts to God. We do not have to hide anything from God, we can be completely open with him: if we are sad, we share that with God; if we are angry, we need to share that.

- 'People think that when Christians pray we just get a nice cosy feeling inside. There is nothing very cosy about standing before your Maker.' (Natalie, 15, quoted in C. Mercier, *Christianity for Today*)

- When we worship someone, we mean that we place great 'worth' on them, acknowledging their 'worthship'. Worship is at the heart of all prayer. Christians base their approach to prayer and worship on what Jesus did.

- The New Testament shows us that Jesus prayed frequently and set aside special times to pray. The Gospels tell us that he often woke early and went away to a quiet place to spend time alone with God. At other times, he would go to the synagogue (the Jewish house of prayer) to join in communal prayer and worship.

- The Christian practice of regular prayer (the clergy pray twice a day at least, and monks and nuns more frequently) and meeting in church for worship reflects Jesus' life.

- Whenever he had a big decision to make, Jesus prayed. Just before he was betrayed by Judas, he prayed in the Garden of Gethsemane, asking God whether he should 'drink the cup of suffering' and die. 'Abba, Father,' he said, 'everything is possible for you. Take this cup from me. Yet not what I will, but what you will.'

- Jesus prays to God as a son speaks to his father, asking only to do his will. The main purpose of Christian prayer, therefore,

➔ *page 54*

# Styles of worship

If you went to a communion service in a hospital you would not expect it to be the same as a grand service with professional choir in a cathedral. Different places and occasions call for different styles of worship and levels of formality.

---

*. . . more Christian beliefs about prayer and worship*

is to align our will with God's, as Jesus did. To do this we need to listen to God. There is an old Christian saying that 'God has given you two ears and one mouth that you may listen twice as much as you speak to him.'

● When we pray, we should open our hearts and minds to him just as Jesus did. There is no need to hide anything from him. We can reveal sadness, joy and anger to him. In fact, Jesus teaches us that our 'Father knows what you need before you ask him.'

● We are not on our own as we pray. The Holy Spirit helps us. As St Paul writes in his letter to the Romans, 'the Spirit helps us in our weakness; for we do not know how to pray as we ought' (Romans 8.26).

● Christians need both private and public prayer and worship. When we pray and worship on our own, we are building up our individual relationship with God. But, as Christians, we are part of the Church, often called 'the Body of Christ' or 'the People of God', and we support one another by praying and worshipping together. Just as in the life of a well-ordered family, we need times on our own and times together.

● Setting a time aside to be with God helps a person to gain a perspective on life. Today everyone is so busy and rushed that it is easy to get caught up in the rat race. Prayer provides time to see things the way God sees them, to see the world through his eyes.

---

But there is also variety in the Anglican Church which stems from differences of belief and attitude. At the time of the Reformation in the sixteenth century, some people would have liked to see the Church of England become more Protestant and others regretted that it could not have been more Roman Catholic. The history since then is very involved but as a very broad generalization, this tension has remained in the Church of England, and throughout much of the worldwide Anglican Communion. Those of a more *Protestant* or '*Low*' (i.e. having a low view of the importance of bishops, priesthood and sacraments) approach tend to prefer simpler worship and those of a more *Catholic* (often called 'Anglo-Catholic') or '*High*' (i.e. those who value bishops, priesthood and sacraments highly) approach prefer more elaborate services, with beautiful vestments, choral singing and incense. This difference is most noticeable at the Eucharist, which the more Protestant Anglicans see principally as a memorial of the Last Supper and the more Catholic regard as making Christ mystically present (see Chapter 14, 'The Eucharist').

Sometimes there is vigorous controversy between the different approaches but many Anglicans are glad that our Church is broad enough to include such variety. You may well find that you are happy to move around sampling different styles. Often whether we prefer one style or another depends upon our temperament and what we are used to.

# Do I have to go to church to be a Christian?

A man was invited to eat a meal by his friend, a priest. When they had eaten, they got talking about prayer and the man asked the priest whether it was necessary to pray and worship with other people. Instead of replying with an argument, the priest told the man to watch what he did. He leaned forward, picked up the tongs and removed a red-hot coal from the fire. It gradually became dark and cool. Then he replaced it among the other lumps of coal. Quickly it became hot and bright again, and the whole fire burned slightly brighter.

# The Christian Calendar

Christians remind themselves of the main parts of Christian teaching by observing an annual cycle of seasons and festivals called the Christian Calendar. The Birth of Jesus is recalled at Christmas; his temptations in the wilderness in Lent; his entry into Jerusalem, the Last Supper, Crucifixion and Resurrection at Easter; his Ascension and the gift of the Holy Spirit creating the Church at Ascension and Pentecost. We also commemorate the Holy Trinity on the Sunday after Pentecost and other events in the life of Jesus, Mary, the Apostles and saints on a variety of feast and saints' days.

There are many ceremonies and customs associated with these. For example, at Christmas, we sing carols and have a crib; during Lent, Christians give up something to commemorate Jesus' fast for 40 days in the wilderness; on Palm Sunday, we carry palms in procession; on Good Friday, the Cross is honoured; and a bonfire and

## THE CHURCH'S YEAR

The Church follows a cycle of festivals and seasons which enable it to retell the story of Jesus and Christianity every year.

**Advent** ................. Four Sundays before Christmas – marking the beginning of the Church Year

**Christmas Day** ....... The celebration of the Birth of Christ, 25 December

**Epiphany** .............. 12 days after Christmas, 6 January, marking the Wise Men's visit to the infant Jesus

**Candlemas** ........... 40 days after Christmas, 2 February, marking the Presentation of Jesus in the Temple

**Shrove Tuesday** ...... The day before Lent begins

**Ash Wednesday** ..... The first day of Lent, 40 days before Easter Day (excluding Sundays), commemorating Jesus' time of fasting in the wilderness

**Palm Sunday** ......... The Sunday before Easter, which begins Holy Week and commemorates Jesus' entry into Jerusalem

**Maundy Thursday** .. The First Day of the Triduum, the Great Three Days preceding Easter Day, commemorating the Last Supper

**Good Friday** ......... The Second Day of the Triduum, commemorating the Crucifixion

**Holy Saturday** ........ The Third Day of the Triduum, when Christ's time in the tomb is commemorated; during the evening Vigil of Easter begins. This ends with the lighting of the Paschal Fire

**Easter Day** ............ The celebration of Christ's Resurrection

**Ascension Day** ....... Marks the Ascension of Christ into heaven and the end of the 40 days of Easter

**Pentecost** ............. Marks the gift of the Holy Spirit to the disciples 50 days after Easter Day. (Pentecost is Greek for 50.)

**Trinity Sunday** ....... Celebrates the doctrine of the Trinity

*Note:* there are many saints' days throughout the Christian Year, e.g. St Peter's Day on 29 June. Easter's date is variable as are its related seasons and festivals (Lent, Ascension, Pentecost, etc.).

*Almost everyone is moved to prayer.*

Paschal (Easter) Candle are lit to mark the Resurrection.

The vestments worn by the clergy and the frontals (coverings on the front of the altars) change according to the 'season' of the Church's Calendar. White or gold is used for festivals of Jesus, Mary and the saints (apart from the martyrs); purple is used for Advent and Lent; red for Pentecost and martyrs; and green for the rest of the year.

## A practical approach to private prayer and public worship

- Anyone can start praying at any time, but do ask someone experienced to help you practically. Ask your priest for advice.

- You should try to establish a habit of prayer and worship. As with everything else, commitment and practice help. You should try to pray every day (even if this is only very brief) and you should try to go to church every week (for most people this will be on a Sunday).

- Experiment with different styles of service so that you find what works best for you at the moment. But bear in mind that this may change as time goes by.

- To begin praying we need to be still and silent. If we are quiet, we can hear God. Praying involves listening to God as well as speaking to him.

- While belonging to a worshipping community helps us to keep going with prayer (see the story above), there will be times when we will want, or have, to pray alone. No one apart from God needs to know that you are praying. You can be sitting on a train, going to work or school, and you can still pray.

*I remember taking a service in Oxford Prison and having to give a talk at rather short notice. I spoke about how we could pray without anyone knowing. I was aware that many of the inmates listening would find it very difficult if their fellows knew that they were praying. (Obviously, they wouldn't be able to kneel by their beds at night, like a small child saying its prayers.) So I said that they could just be lying on their bunks first thing in the morning or last thing at night, when everyone else was asleep, and still pray quietly to God.*

*A friend of mine, who was the prison chaplain, visited the prison the next day. One of the young men he spoke to had just had an appendicitis operation and was feeling very low and depressed. He told my friend what a difference it had made to him to hear 'that bloke we had yesterday' saying that you could pray so simply that no one else even needed to know.*

- Some practical things can help you to pray, though. Set prayers, especially if you memorize them, can give you something to repeat aloud or to yourself to settle the mind. You can use the Lord's Prayer in this way, praying it slowly, line by line, with pauses for meditation in between.

- You may like to choose a room or place where you can be quiet. Some people have a cross or picture of Jesus to focus on when they begin praying. Or perhaps they light a candle and focus on it as they pray. Obviously, your parish church or a chapel within it could be a good place if it's easy to get to and open regularly. But you will also want to establish a place in your own home and a time when it is convenient.

- The way you sit or kneel can help, especially if you are going to pray for some time. Try sitting upright in a chair which allows your feet to touch the ground. Rest your hands on the armrests or on your knees. Breathe slowly in and out, becoming aware of your breaths as you pray. (There are many guides to prayer which go into far more detail than we can here.) You may also find it helpful to use a rosary to order your meditation.

● If you pray with others in a group, you will be able to help each other.

# THINKING IT THROUGH

⧗ Which do you think would be the best time to set aside for prayer?

⧗ What do you think you are doing when you pray?

⧗ What does it mean to listen to God in prayer? How does God speak to people? Do you expect to hear a voice or does God communicate through other means?

⧗ How would you respond to someone who said that God does not answer prayer because he does not heal everyone who is sick and prays?

⧗ C. S. Lewis said he prayed because he needed to. What do you think he meant? Do you agree with him?

## BIBLE STUDY

Matthew 6.9–13

Matthew's gospel provides the longer version of the Lord's Prayer. Apart from being the most famous Christian prayer, it also reminds us of the need to pray simply.

# FOR PRAYER & REFLECTION

*Almighty and everlasting God,*
*you are always more ready to hear than*
 *we to pray*
*and to give more than either we desire or*
 *deserve:*
*pour down upon us the abundance of your*
 *mercy,*
*forgiving us those things of which our*
 *conscience is afraid*
*and giving us those good things which we*
 *are not worthy to ask*
*but through the merits and mediation*
 *of Jesus Christ your Son our Lord.*

## SOME PRAYER TOPICS . . .

❖ Ask God to help you pray.

❖ Pray through a newspaper. Carefully select two or three articles to read. After each one take time to reflect prayerfully on people in the story – offer each person up to God. Also learn to pray over the TV news – offer up quick 'arrow' prayers as you watch.

❖ Go through the past week in your mind and thank God for all that has happened. 'Lord, teach us to worship you throughout the day.'

*Lighting candles or other outward gestures often accompany and assist prayer.*

# $T$HE SACRAMENTS

## What is a sacrament?

### A sacrament is symbolic

Desmond Morris trained as a zoologist but later turned his attention to humans. He travelled to over sixty countries to examine human behaviour. 'Instead of listening to what people said,' he writes in his book *Manwatching*, 'I would observe what they did . . . like a birdwatcher. I would become a man-watcher . . . Each one of us uses our hands as signalling devices every day of our lives. One of the best locations to study hand gestures is a political rally. If he [the political speaker] is making a powerful point, he will clench his fist, as if about to punch an invisible opponent.'

Desmond Morris gathered evidence to demonstrate how humans use their bodies to communicate inner meanings – how they think and feel. Many of our gestures, he showed, are symbolic. They help us to express ourselves when we find it difficult to put our feelings and thoughts into words.

For Christians, the seven sacraments provide special ceremonies and gestures to communicate their deepest religious thoughts and feelings at key moments in their lives.

*We use our bodies in a variety of ways to communicate with each other. Each of us has our own body language. What are the people in the photograph saying?*

### A sacrament points to God

Have you noticed how many commercial adverts (for example, for cars, chocolates, etc.) also contain shots of handsome, rich people in beautiful houses? These adverts are designed to suggest that if you buy the product on offer you too can take part in a dream world. The product becomes a symbol pointing to something else.

The same is the case with a sacrament. A sacrament should not just be seen from the outside. It should also be seen as

# Christian beliefs about the sacraments

- **Sacraments are central to the worship of the Church.** In the oldest tradition of the Church, the word *sacrament* was used for everything to do with the sacred. In the twelfth century the Church pinpointed seven sacraments. They are ceremonies or rituals: two can be traced back to the time of Jesus (Baptism and the Eucharist); the other five can be traced back to the early Church (confirmation; confession; marriage; ordination; anointing of the sick).

- **A sacrament is an outward sign of an invisible grace.** The best known definition of sacrament is that given by St Augustine (AD 354–430): 'A sacrament is the visible form of an invisible grace.' Another way of defining a sacrament is to say that it is a signpost pointing to God, or a dramatization of something which is happening spiritually within a person. As both of these definitions indicate, there are two parts to a sacrament:

  (1) A visible part – something material is used in a sacrament. For example, at baptism water is poured over the candidate's forehead; at the Eucharist people eat bread and wine; when the sick are anointed oil is used. The material things focus on the reality of God's presence in a uniquely appropriate way: water in baptism expresses the washing away of sin, and the bread and wine of the Eucharist express the body and blood of Jesus.

  (2) The spiritual or invisible part – God comes close to the worshipper through the physical elements. In each sacrament God gives the Holy Spirit to encourage and strengthen the worshipper.

- **We need to have faith when we receive the sacraments.** They are not magic. We have to receive them believing in the gift that God is giving us through them.

- **A number of the sacraments mark out important developments in a person's life.** Entry into the Church, as a baby, child or adult, is marked by baptism; movement from unconscious to conscious faith is marked by confirmation; the commitment to a partner for life is marked by marriage. Confession and reconciliation mark the restoration of the sinner to a right relationship with God; ordination marks a change of life to a calling to serve God and people as a bishop, priest or deacon; and anointing marks progress from sickness to health or, in a final illness, from this life to the next.

- **Christians believe that the meaning of *sacrament* is most fully expressed in Jesus himself.** He is God (the invisible and spiritual grace) who became human flesh (the visible and outward sign).

- **The sacraments both express change in people's lives and also make change happen.** For example, a wedding expresses the changed perception people have of their relationship but they also feel and are different after their wedding. This is something other people recognize as marriage brings about a changed role and status in society.

pointing to something else hidden 'inside', at the spiritual level. So, in the sacrament of the Eucharist, the bread and wine are simply bread and wine looked at from the outside but from the 'inside' they also point to the presence of Christ in the world.

Everything is, or can become, a sacrament. For St Francis of Assisi, for example, everything spoke of God – the lambs in the field, the flowers, even fire and death. The whole world became a sacrament pointing to God.

# Why seven sacraments?

If everything can be sacramental, we might well ask why the Church has only seven sacraments.

The answer is that each of the seven sacraments celebrates a turning point in a person's life where God is experienced in a major way (e.g. baptism, confirmation – becoming a Christian adult, etc.).

## The Seven Sacraments

Baptism
Confirmation
The Eucharist
Marriage
Confession
Ordination
Anointing the Sick

Only baptism and the Eucharist are described in the Bible. Each of the seven sacraments is explained in detail in the chapters which follow.

## THINKING IT THROUGH

⧗ Is there anything in your life which especially speaks of God to you? It could be a place, a person, or a happening in the past. Such things can have sacramental value.

⧗ Many Christians would say that a priest's main job is to administer the sacraments. Why do you think that they say this?

*Each one of us uses our hands as signalling devices every day of our lives.*

# *B*APTISM

*In a service of baptism (or of baptism and confirmation) the Church proclaims what God has done for his people in Christ and offers us a way of entering that movement from darkness to light, from death to life, from being self-centred to being God-centred.*

To your parents, your baptism probably seemed a very natural way of thanking God for your birth and asking him for his protection and help while you were growing up.

But we need to be aware that baptism is a very brave step to take in some parts of the world. As Charles Colson has written, 'Most Westerners take baptism for granted, but for many in the world the act requires immense courage. In countries like Nepal it once meant imprisonment. For Soviet or Chinese or Eastern bloc believers, it was like signing their own death warrant' (*The Body*).

*The baptism service often takes place around a special baptismal font near the entrance to the church. Baptism represents the entry of a person into the Christian faith.*

## What happens at baptism?

- Baptism normally takes place at a public Sunday service. However, it can also take place in a private service for the family.

- The priest greets the person to be baptized. Those old enough to make promises on their own behalf will be accompanied by sponsors. If the person to receive baptism is a baby, the parents and godparents will be welcomed.

- The service provides an opportunity to express thanksgiving. 'The Liturgy of the Word and the sermon are an opportunity to set the story of what God has done in Christ alongside our own story', as the introduction to the revised services puts it. We are encouraged to see a connection between the story of Christ and our own experience.

- This leads to the presentation of those to be baptized and their welcome by the congregation. Together they (or, in the case of the very young, the parents and godparents on their behalf) accept their 'shared responsibility for their growth in faith'.

- This in turn leads to a 'solemn renunciation' (rejection) 'of evil and the expression of a desire to follow Christ'.

- At this point, those to be baptized are recognized as being part of 'the believing community' and are reminded of the cost of following Jesus as disciples. The priest then makes the sign of the cross on their foreheads. This is the 'badge of the pilgrim community', the sign that they are prepared to commit themselves to follow Jesus from now until the end of their lives.

- The congregation then moves to the font. This is a large basin which is often found close to the entrance of the church. Just as people physically enter the church through the door, they spiritually enter the Church, the body of believers in Christ, by means of baptism.

- Those to be baptized – or, if they are too young, their parents and godparents – then 'express their longing for the transforming grace of God's Holy Spirit in the Prayer over the Water'. They join together in saying the Creed, which shows that they are at one with the community of those who already believe.

- Then they go alone (or are carried) to the waters of the font to be baptized. They are supported by others 'embracing Christ's dying and rising' but it is also a very personal and individual experience, just like each person's birth and death. 'Alone, we pass from death to life, leaving sin and self drowned in the waters, from which we rise to a new life that is Christ's and shared with all the baptized.'

- A new life has begun, which is 'directed and empowered by the Spirit'. This recalls the way in which the Spirit 'overshadowed Jesus as he came up from the waters of baptism'. As a sign of this, those who have been baptized may be clothed in special white clothes (symbolizing purification) and anointed (as a 'sign of their belonging with all the baptized in the royal priesthood of God's holy people').

- They are then commissioned to live out the baptized life and (if they are old enough) to take part in the prayers of the Church and 'in the action of the Eucharist.'

- Finally, to emphasize that the baptized have a life which 'not only takes place in worship', at the end of the service they are given a lighted candle to show that they have a mission to take Christ's light out into the world. This is lit from the Easter (Paschal) candle, which is a symbol of Christ's resurrection and victory over evil and death. They are told to 'Shine as a light in the world to the glory of God the Father.'

# The meaning of baptism

Jesus began his preaching and healing ministry by being baptized in the river Jordan. The vast majority of his followers over the two thousand years since then have begun their Christian lives with baptism.

*Today Christians can still be baptized in the river Jordan. Many Christians go on pilgrimage to the Holy Land to be baptized in the same river as Jesus.*

In the Anglican Church many people get baptized when they are babies. However, when people convert to Christianity as an adult they can receive adult baptism. It is a once-and-for-all sacrament – it cannot be redone or undone.

There are several ways to understand baptism.

## An act of cleansing

Have you ever stood under a waterfall? Even standing under a very powerful shower can make you feel as though your breath is being taken away. The word 'baptism' comes from the Greek word meaning to dip or immerse in water. During the service of baptism the priest will pour water over the person being baptized or plunge them under it. Water is a powerful symbol to show how Christ washes away a person's sins and gives them a new fresh start.

There is a saying that when people want to make a fresh start at something (for example, they decide to stop swearing) they are 'turning over a new leaf'. Christians believe that baptism is a sign that a person has turned over a new leaf, to start living a completely new life for God. It marks the beginning of the Christian journey through life. However, it is just the beginning of something, it is not like a good luck charm for life. It has to be followed by living as a Christian.

*Baptism is a purifying, a making clean.*

## An act of identity

Do you wear a school uniform? If you do you are identifying yourself with the school that you attend. However, an act of identity is not always a matter of the clothes you wear. Sometimes it involves the things which you do.

A Christian is someone who identifies with Jesus Christ. The way in which Christians may do this varies from person to person (for example, some people wear a cross around their neck). However, there is one act of identity which is common to all Christians. It is baptism. St Paul talks about baptism as being 'clothed, so to speak, with the life of Christ himself' (Galatians 3.27). The language symbolizes the stripping off of the clothes of sin (old habits) and putting on new clothes of Christ at baptism: 'you have taken off the old self with its habits and have put on the new self' (Colossians 3.9–10).

## An act of belonging

Think of the clubs/societies you are a member of or would like to join. What entrance requirements do you need to fulfil in order to belong to these clubs? Why do clubs and organizations have entrance requirements?

Baptism is an outward sign that a person belongs to God's Church Family. During the service the person being baptized is welcomed by the rest of the church with the following words: 'We welcome you into the fellowship of faith;
we are children of the same heavenly Father;
we welcome you.'

## An initiation ceremony

Baptism is also a new beginning. It marks the beginning of your membership of the Church.

Baptism means being united to the death and resurrection of Jesus. It means we are asked to 'die' to our old, sinful self, and grow up as a new person in the light of Christ. It is also a promise that when we die, we will share the eternal life of Jesus.

*Who are the people in the photograph identifying themselves with? Why have they painted themselves like this? Imagine that you have been invited to an international fancy dress party where you are expected to identify with your country. Suggest ways in which you might do this.*

*What are the requirements for belonging to clubs like this?*

In the Anglican Church when babies are baptized they become part of God's Church Family. Augustine, one of the Church Fathers, compared what happens at baptism to the mark or seal that in Augustine's day was tattooed on a soldier to show who was his lord and master. Baptism is a mark that God is the lord of the child's life. When an adult converts to Christianity in their baptism they promise to turn around from their old way of life and to follow Christ.

Another name for baptism is *christening*. This is sometimes called Christianing – being made a Christian. The person receives the Holy Spirit into their life. Frequently, anointing with *chrism* (oil mixed with fragrant spices) is used as a sign of the blessings brought by the Holy Spirit. At the anointing, the ancient Chi-Rho sign (which consists of the first two letters in Greek of the name of 'Christ', i.e. 'Anointed one') may be made on the forehead of the person who has been baptized.

## A death and a resurrection

In the early days of Christianity baptism was normally intended for adults and was performed at Easter time. Jesus called his death and resurrection a 'baptism'. To his apostles he said: 'Are you willing to be baptized with the baptism with which I must be baptized?' St Paul used the image of dying and rising to new life to explain the meaning of baptism: 'We have died to sin . . . by our baptism we were buried with him [Jesus] and shared his death, in order that, just as Christ was raised from death . . . so also we might live a new life . . . we know that our old being has been put to death with Christ on his cross, in order that the power of the sinful self might be destroyed, so that we should no longer be the slaves of sin'

> ## DECISION
>
> *A large candle may be lit. The president addresses the candidates directly, or through their parents, godparents and sponsors.*
>
> In baptism, God calls us out of darkness into his marvellous light.
>
> To follow Christ means dying to sin and rising to new life with him.
>
> Therefore I ask:
>
> Do you reject the devil and all rebellion against God?
>
> *I reject them.*
>
> Do you renounce the deceit and corruption of evil?
>
> *I renounce them.*
>
> Do you repent of the sins that separate us from God and neighbour?
>
> *I repent of them.*
>
> Do you turn to Christ as Saviour?
>
> *I turn to Christ.*
>
> Do you submit to Christ as Lord?
>
> *I submit to Christ.*
>
> Do you come to Christ, the way, the truth and the life?
>
> *I come to Christ.*

(Romans 6.2, 4, 6). Paul means that all our lives long we are struggling to leave behind our old, natural life of sin and selfishness, to try and grow more like Christ. He also sees baptism as a guarantee that when this life is over we will share with Christ in eternal life.

*I did not get baptized as a baby, but when I was 21. I wanted to make a new beginning and let Jesus rule my life from now on. (Carrie)*

At baptism the child receives the gift of the Holy Spirit. From earliest times the giving of the Holy Spirit has been associated with baptism (Acts 8.14–17).

It is the Holy Spirit which leads us to grow in faith as we journey on our pilgrimage through life. This is reflected in this prayer from the baptism service:

> *May God, who has received you by baptism into his Church,*
> *pour upon you the riches of his grace,*
> *that within the company of Christ's pilgrim people*
> *you may daily be renewed by his anointing Spirit,*
> *and come to the inheritance of the saints in glory. Amen.*

## THINKING IT THROUGH

⧗ Why do you think that the whole church might turn out to see a new Christian being baptized? Why is baptism so important?

⧗ What is the symbolic meaning of the following in the baptism service: pouring water over the person's head; making the sign of the cross on the person's head; anointing with chrism; giving the person a lighted candle? Why is the candle lit from the Easter candle?

⧗ Often parents ask for baptism for their baby because they think it is a nice celebration or because the grand-parents want it. Do you think these are good enough reasons? Do you think the Church should baptize children of parents who are not Christians?

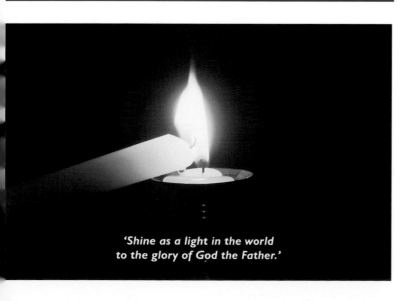

**'Shine as a light in the world to the glory of God the Father.'**

# BIBLE STUDY

Read the story of Jesus' baptism at the beginning of Matthew's Gospel (Matthew 3.13–17).

Jesus goes down to the river Jordan where he is baptized by John the Baptist. The Holy Spirit descends upon him and a voice comes from heaven declaring that Jesus is God's beloved Son.

- ◆ Why was John the Baptist reluctant to baptize Jesus?

- ◆ What does the voice of God tell us about Jesus' importance?

- ◆ Why do you think that Jesus was tempted by the devil immediately after his baptism?

## FOR PRAYER & REFLECTION

*God of Glory,*
*you inspire us with the breath of life*
*which brought to birth a new world in Christ.*
*May we who are reborn in him*
*be transformed by the renewal of our lives,*
*that the light of your new creation*
*may flood the world with your abundant grace;*
*through Christ our Lord.*

*Amen.*

## SOME PRAYER TOPICS . . .

❖ For help in turning to Christ.

❖ To be able to repent of our sins each day.

❖ To fight against evil in our lives and in the world.

# Chapter 13

# CONFIRMATION

At your confirmation the Bishop will say:

*'Brothers and sisters, I ask you to profess together with these candidates the faith of the Church.'*

## Standing up for what you believe

As children grow up they often adopt the beliefs, opinions and ideas of their parents. However, during adolescence they start to develop their own personalities and acquire individual likes and dislikes, beliefs and values. Teenage years have been described as times of rebellion because youngsters often rebel against their parents (and other authority figures). Sometimes this is done peacefully and is marked by teenagers choosing their own styles of clothes etc.; at other times it can lead to conflict, as the wishes of children clash with those of their parents.

**Why do you think teenage years have been described as years of rebellion?**

This transition from someone being a child to being an adult is a time for people to stand up for what they believe. As a teenager gets older they are given more freedom (e.g. to stay out later, to be able to buy cigarettes when they are 16, or alcoholic drink when they are 18, or to drive a car). But at the same time they have to take on more responsibility for their actions.

Within Christianity this transition to taking adult responsibility is marked by the sacrament of confirmation – it is a time when young people confirm for themselves the promises which their parents and godparents made for them at their baptism. Confirmation involves taking responsibility for your religious faith. It is a time when you yourself publicly declare that you want to belong to the Church. You do this by making a profession (formal statement) of faith before the Bishop, who serves as a representative of the universal Church. It is also a time when people receive the gifts of the Holy Spirit in a special way.

However, confirmation is not just something for teenagers. Many adults become confirmed later on in their life – they may have been baptized as a baby but then throughout their life they have not grown up in the Christian faith. Later they come back to the Church and want to make a public affirmation of their faith.

# The meaning of confirmation

## Being an ambassador

An ambassador is someone who represents his or her country abroad. They have to represent their country's beliefs and values, and speak out on its behalf.

When Christians are confirmed they reconfirm the promises which their parents and godparents made for them at baptism. They take on the responsibility for themselves to represent Christ in the world. They are Christ's ambassadors – they are God's co-workers in the world.

*In what sense are these pupils ambassadors for their school? What responsibilities do they have? Should this affect the way they act?*

# Christian beliefs about confirmation

- In the early Church baptism and the 'laying on of hands' were performed on adult converts (Acts 8.17; 19.6). However, the two acts of baptism and 'laying on of hands' became separate in the Western Church as they began to baptize at the Easter Vigil in parishes where the Bishop was not present. The laying on of hands by the Bishop then had to wait until it could be performed later in the sacrament of confirmation.

- **Confirmation continues what was begun at baptism.** Confirmation celebrates the presence and work of the Holy Spirit within us. It also marks full membership of the Church.

- **Confirmation classes.** To prepare a person for confirmation the priest will hold confirmation classes in which he will instruct confirmation candidates into what it means to accept the Christian faith and to live as a Christian in the world. Confirmation classes might last for a few months or up to a year.

- **The confirmation service is led by the Bishop.** He represents the universal Church. This emphasizes the importance of confirmation. It starts with the people being confirmed renewing their baptismal promises – which were made on their behalf by their parents and godparents if they were baptized as infants – and agreeing to take responsibility for them. The Bishop will say: 'Are you ready with your own mouth and from your own heart to affirm your faith in Jesus Christ?'

- **The confirmation candidates make a profession of faith.** They do this by uniting with the congregation in saying the Apostles' Creed.

- **The Bishop asks the Holy Spirit to come and rest upon the confirmation candidates.** At the heart of this sacrament, as all sacraments, is the giving of God's power,

➜ page 70

his Holy Spirit. The Bishop stretches his hands towards the confirmation candidates and prays that they will be given the sevenfold gifts of the Holy Spirit (see the prayer at the end of this chapter).

● **The Bishop addresses each candidate by name**, saying, 'God has called you by name and made you his own.' He then lays his hand on each, saying, 'Confirm, O Lord, your servant with your Holy Spirit.' The congregation then pray with him, asking that the candidates may 'daily increase in' the Holy Spirit more and more. The laying on of hands by the Bishop reflects the custom of the apostles, who laid on hands when they prayed for someone to receive special gifts (Acts 13.1–3).

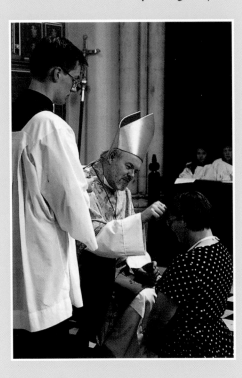

*The Bishop anoints a candidate with the oil of chrism during a confirmation service.*

● **Chrism, oil mixed with fragrant spices, may accompany confirmation.** This expresses the richness of the Holy Spirit. The word *chrism*, like *Christ*, comes from the Greek word meaning 'to anoint'. From Old Testament times prophets, priests and kings have been anointed with oil, as a sign of the Spirit empowering them to fulfil their special calling. Now God anoints you with his Spirit, to enable you to fulfil the special work he wants you to do for him in your Christian life.

● **The confirmation candidates then receive the Eucharist.**

## Taking a stand can be costly

In Russia under communism attempts were made to destroy the Christian faith. Here is a letter from a Christian schoolgirl in Lithuania:

> *When I was in fifth form the class teacher tried to force me to join the Pioneers – the communist youth movement. When he saw me hesitate he said: 'If you refuse this year, next year you'll have to.' As later on I still refused he threatened me with bad marks and other punishments. My marks from some of the teachers got worse and worse.*
>
> (Quoted in P. Lefevre, *One Hundred Stories to Change Your Life*)

Although being a Christian in England does not bring such punishments as this it can still be a costly business.

> *Sometimes I find it difficult standing up for what I believe. It can make me unpopular with my friends especially when they want to do something which I disagree with. They start to say that I am no fun. It would be so much easier sometimes to follow the crowd.* (James)

## THINKING IT THROUGH

⧗ Have you ever had to stand up for what you believe in? Have you ever found yourself in a situation in which following God looks like the most difficult way?

⧗ What do you think is meant by the promise a confirmation candidate makes to reject all that is evil? Make a list of things which you may need to reject. Think about which area of your life is most difficult to give totally to God.

⧗ Do you think there is an ideal age at which to be confirmed?

## BIBLE STUDY

Read Galatians 5.16–25. This is one of the suggested readings for the confirmation service.

♦ Paul starts by describing a battle going on within the person. Inside us there is a pull to do what we know is wrong. We are often disappointed because our best efforts are not enough to make us better than we are. Try to provide examples of what Paul might be referring to when he talks about 'our human nature' and 'what the Spirit wants' (verses 16–18).

♦ According to Paul what sort of behaviour is to be avoided as you grow in the Christian life (verses 19–21)? Why do you think these things are to be avoided?

♦ In this passage Paul goes on to describe the marks of a Christian life which are produced by the Holy Spirit working in you. What qualities does he refer to (verses 22–26)?

## FOR PRAYER & REFLECTION

*When the Bishop stretches out his hands over you at your confirmation he will say the following prayer asking for you to receive the sevenfold gifts of the Holy Spirit:*

*Almighty and ever-living God,*

*you have given these your servants new birth*

*in baptism by water and the Spirit,*

*and have forgiven them all their sins.*

*Let your Holy Spirit rest upon them:*

*the Spirit of wisdom and understanding;*

*the Spirit of counsel and inward strength;*

*the Spirit of knowledge and true godliness;*

*and let their delight be in the fear of the Lord.*

*Amen.*

*After confirmation the following prayer is said by the whole congregation:*

*Defend, O Lord, these your servants with your heavenly grace,*

*that they may continue yours for ever,*

*and daily increase in your Holy Spirit more and more*

*until they come to your everlasting kingdom.*

*Amen.*

## SOME PRAYER TOPICS . . .

❖ For inward strength to stand up for your beliefs.

❖ For guidance in understanding God's will for your life.

❖ For help in living the Christian life, and showing forth the qualities of the Holy Spirit within you.

# *T*HE EUCHARIST

*. . . as we eat and drink these holy gifts*

*in the presence of your divine majesty,*

*renew us by your Holy Spirit*

*and nourish us with the body and blood*

*of Christ,*

*that we may grow into his likeness.*

I know someone in her late seventies who is a grandmother. She wears several rings on her left hand, including a simple gold one which is very old. It belonged to her mother and her mother's mother in turn. She has worn it for thirty years, as did her mother. It has many associations, in fact it's the only really personal thing of her mother's which she has. It is virtually indistinguishable from dozens of other gold rings but for her it would be irreplaceable as it helps to keep the memory of her mother alive.

For Christians, the Eucharist is something precious and irreplaceable. It gives them a unique way of being close to Jesus.

## What happens at the Eucharist?

The style of services varies considerably. As we said on page 54, some will be grand services, like a coronation, and others very simple – imagine an army chaplain giving communion to soldiers living under canvas. Also, some services will have a lot of ritual (bells, incense, etc.) and others very little. Some will use communion 'wafers', others a simple loaf of bread. In some churches, elaborate vestments (ceremonial clothes) will be worn and in others the clergy will wear their ordinary clothes.

All Anglican Churches authorize at least one and usually more forms of service for the celebration of the Eucharist, some in modern language, and some more traditional. All these forms of service fall into four main parts: the Ministry of the Word; Thanksgiving of the Community; the Ministry of the Sacrament; and the Sending Out.

*Sometimes the Eucharist is celebrated in formal services. At other times, as in this picture, it can take place within an informal service – for example, in a house or at a youth group. Sometimes an ordinary loaf of bread is used.*

## Ministry of the Word

*Greeting* by the priest – having gathered together, the people are greeted by the priest.

*Penitence*: in preparation to hear God's Word, they confess their sins and receive absolution.

*Gloria and Kyries*: these will be used according to the season of the Church's Year (e.g. the Gloria is not sung in Lent); they are not generally used when the Eucharist is celebrated on a weekday.

*Collect*: there are special prayers for each week in the Church's calendar and for saints' days. These are intended to introduce the readings.

*Bible readings*: from both the Old and the New Testaments, concluding with a Gospel reading, for which all stand. There may be three, two or – rarely – only one reading, but there is always a reading from the Gospel.

*Sermon*: to explain and teach about the readings.

*The Creed* – the Nicene Creed, a statement of what Christians believe, may be said by everyone but it is not used at every service.

## Thanksgiving of the Community

*Intercessions*: the prayers and thanksgiving of the people will be offered. These may follow a set form or be written for the particular service.

# Christian beliefs about the Eucharist

**What is happening? Why do you think this is important to the people who are present?**

- Anglicans all over the world, like the great majority of Christians, meet to repeat an action which Jesus performed with his disciples on the night before he died. **For many Christians the Eucharist is the most important act of worship**: Kings and Queens take part in it after they have been crowned; married couples celebrate it after their wedding; and the dying receive it on their death bed.

- **Jesus celebrated a Last Supper with his disciples on the night before he died.** Ever since then Christians have obeyed Jesus' command to repeat his actions. The Acts of the Apostles tell us how the early Christians met regularly for the 'breaking of the bread' (Acts 2.42). In the Eucharist we often say or sing the canticle 'Lamb of God, you take away the sins of the world'. This reminds us that at the Last Supper, Jesus put himself in the place of the Passover Lamb, and that the Eucharist is our new, Christian Passover meal.

- **The word Eucharist means thanksgiving**: Jesus 'gave thanks' over the bread and wine. When Christians repeat this command they are (a) giving thanks, as Jesus did, for all the good things of nature (represented by the bread and wine); (b) calling to mind what Jesus was about to do (die on the cross) and giving thanks for Jesus' offering; and (c) asking God to make Jesus present again.

➔ *page 76*

*The Ministry of the Word.*

*During the Eucharistic prayer, the bread is blessed and consecrated.*

*In more formal services the priest places a special communion wafer of bread in the hand of the communicant. This is the body of Christ.*

*At the end of the Eucharistic service the priest will bless the congregation and send them out in peace.*

## Ministry of the Sacrament

*The Peace*: a handshake or embrace is exchanged to remind us that Christians make up one body united in mutual love.

*The Eucharistic Prayer*: the president (bishop or priest), in dialogue with the people, recalls God's saving acts, gives thanks over the bread and wine and says the words which Jesus himself said at the Last Supper. The bread and wine are consecrated in this prayer. Some Christians show their reverence for the moment of consecration and the presence of Christ in the sacrament by one of the following actions: bending the right knee (genuflecting); censing (using incense); elevating the bread and wine (lifting them up for people to see); ringing bells.

*The bread is broken (the fraction)*: after the bread has been broken, the president invites the people to receive the Body and Blood of Christ.

In many churches, after the service some of the consecrated bread is placed in a safe called an aumbry or tabernacle, so that it is readily available to be taken to sick people who cannot come to church. A white light burns near the place where the sacrament is 'reserved', usually in a side chapel where people can go for private prayer. Many find such a quiet place very helpful and may genuflect as a sign of reverence.

## The Sending Out

At the end of the service the people, having heard God's Word and having been nourished by Christ's Body and Blood, go out to be witnesses of Christ in the world and to continue his work. The priest blesses them and dismisses them.

# The meaning of the Eucharist

Since the Eucharist is very important and precious to Christians, it is important that we prepare ourselves thoroughly for it. St Paul warns against eating the Lord's Supper without proper preparation (1 Corinthians 11.27–29): we must approach it with the right attitude. We should take going to each Eucharist seriously, which is one of the reasons why the service begins with the confession of sins and asking for God's forgiveness.

The following story shows the importance of the right attitude:

> One day the Emperor Napoleon with one of his servants decided to go out into the town disguised as ordinary citizens. They went to an inn for a meal. At the end of the meal the landlady brought them a bill for 14 francs. They searched in their pockets for money but to their embarrassment found none. They promised to bring back the money within the hour.
>
> The landlady would not hear of it. She threatened to fetch the police if she was not paid at once. The waiter felt sorry for the two gentlemen and offered to pay the bill for them – 'they seem honest men'. So they were able to leave the inn without the police being called.
>
> Within hours the servant returned to the inn and asked the landlady how much she had bought it for. She replied, 30,000 francs, at which point the servant handed the landlady the money for the inn and told her: 'On the emperor's orders I am commanded to present this inn to the waiter who helped him out in his need.'
>
> (Adapted from P. Lefevre, *One Hundred Stories to Change Your Life*)

### . . . more Christian beliefs about the Eucharist

- **The Eucharist unites us to Christ's sacrifice on the cross.** As we receive the Sacrament, we not only remember Jesus' self-offering; we are united with it, and its grace becomes effective in our lives.

- The whole Eucharist reminds us of Jesus' sacrifice on the cross. It was a costly sacrifice **which shows us how much God loves us**, enough for him to send his only Son to die for us.

- At the Eucharist the president (a bishop or priest) repeats Jesus' actions. Everyone gathers around the altar to re-enact the meal which Jesus had with his disciples. The president takes the bread and wine ('*he took*'), says a prayer over them ('*gave thanks*'), breaks it ('*he broke*') and shares it ('*he gave*'). This is called the fourfold action: **taking – giving thanks – breaking – sharing.** All Eucharists, however much their language or ceremony may vary, contain these actions.

- **The meaning of the Eucharist.** Sadly, debate about the meaning of the Eucharist has been one of the main points of division between the denominations. However, after centuries of argument about what Jesus meant by giving us his body and blood (and, in particular, about whether those words should be understood literally or symbolically), there are some encouraging signs of agreement. An important Agreed Statement on the doctrine of the Eucharist has been drawn up by the Anglican–Roman Catholic International Commission, which avoids many of the old controversies, and talks more simply of the real, objective presence of Jesus in the consecrated bread and wine. The World Council of Churches has also produced a statement of Eucharistic doctrine on similar lines. Put simply, it means that in some way we do not fully understand, Jesus really gives himself to us in the community sharing the consecrated bread and wine. The bread and wine are really changed (that is why they must either be consumed or carefully reserved after the service), and become the means of him being present with us and in us.

- **We human beings are not creatures of spirit only:** we are also made of flesh and blood. That's why Jesus himself became incarnate to save us. In a way, Jesus is incarnate in the Eucharist again. He comes not only spiritually but physically, as the consecrated bread and wine. Like all the sacraments, the Eucharist is more than words. Even in an ordinary relationship, a single hug can sometimes mean more than many words. In the Eucharist Jesus gives us this physical expression of his love to express and sustain our relationship with him.

- **This sacrament is known by a number of names.** Apart from **Eucharist**, some Christians refer to it as **Holy Communion**, which draws attention to the belief that Christians meet Christ in the bread and wine and that this celebration takes place in the company of all Christians, and 'with angels and archangels, and with all the company of heaven'. Other Christians call it the **Mass**, which comes from the closing words of the service in its Latin form ('Ite *missa* est' – 'Go, you are sent out into the world'). Strengthened by the meal which we have shared, we are sent out into the world to 'live and work to your praise and glory'.

The landlady and the waiter reacted very differently to the same two men. As a result the landlady lost her inn and the waiter received a rich reward. Christians believe that when they receive Jesus' body and blood in the form of bread and wine it is important that they have the right attitude.

When they have the right attitude, Christians find receiving communion very special:

*When I was confirmed and first took communion I felt very special. Now I feel closer to Jesus when I take his body and blood.* (Emily, 14)

*Once I have received the Eucharist I feel that I have a fresh start – I can go out into the world trying to love others all over again.* (John, 15)

*It is my spiritual food – it gives me strength for all that I have to do in the day.* (Andrea, 24)

*The Eucharist is important to me because I feel that I am closest to my brother who died two years ago. It is a spiritual meal in which we join together with all Christians and the heavenly host.* (James, 18)

We come together in the Body of Christ. We share Holy Communion and are then sent out to carry on the work of Jesus. 'You are the Body of Christ: you are to be taken, consecrated, broken and distributed, that you may be the means of grace' to others (St Augustine).

## THINKING IT THROUGH

⧖ How do you think you should prepare for receiving communion?

⧖ Why do you think the Eucharist is so important to many Christians?

⧖ Some countries do not grow grapes and do not have the raw materials to make bread. What alternatives could Christians use to celebrate the Eucharist?

## BIBLE STUDY

Read the account of the Last Supper in Luke 22.14–23.

On the night before he died Jesus shared a last meal with his closest disciples. The Eucharist is based upon this last supper. During the meal Jesus says a special prayer over the bread and the wine.

◆ What conversation did Jesus have with his disciples during the meal? How did the disciples react to what Jesus said?

◆ Bread and wine were normal everyday foods. What special meaning did Jesus give to the bread and to the wine?

◆ The bread was broken. What does this point to? The wine was poured. What does this pouring refer to?

## FOR PRAYER & REFLECTION

*Almighty God,*
*we thank you for feeding us*
*with the body and blood of your Son Jesus Christ.*
*Through him we offer you our souls and bodies*
*to be a living sacrifice.*
*Send us out*
*in the power of your Spirit*
*to live and work*
*to your praise and glory.*
　　　　*Amen.*

## SOME PRAYER TOPICS . . .

❖ Ask God to make our hearts pure so that we can come to celebrate the Eucharist.

❖ Ask God to forgive us our sins – to give us a new start.

❖ Thank Jesus for his willingness to have his body broken on the cross and his blood poured out – for showing his love for us.

❖ Ask God that through the Eucharist he will give us his spiritual food – to strengthen us in our faith by his Holy Spirit.

# Chapter 15

# MARRIAGE

*Marriage is a gift of God in creation
through which husband and wife may
know the grace of God.
It is given that as man and woman
grow together in love and trust,
they shall be united with one another in
heart, body and mind,
as Christ is united with his bride, the
Church.*

Can you see yourself getting married?
What do you think marriage is and why
do people decide to take marriage vows
instead of just living together?

Fifty or so years ago most people got
married in church. But today a growing
number of people are deciding against
marriage. Are there good reasons for
getting married or do you think that
marriage is out of date?

## What happens at a wedding service?

- The priest welcomes everybody
  present and reminds them of the
  reasons for marriage.

- Bible passages (usually on the theme
  of love and marriage) are read and a
  sermon is preached.

- Bride and groom declare their
  intention and the congregation is
  asked if they will support them.

- The bride and groom exchange vows
  with each other: 'to have and to hold

## Marriage rates hit 150-year low

Marriage rates have fallen to their
lowest level since records began
150 years ago, while divorce rates
have risen to a new peak, a report
shows.

Sixty per cent of couples live
together before their wedding day,
compared with 6 per cent in the
1960s.

*During the marriage
service the union of
husband and wife is
blessed by God.*

from this day forward; for better, for worse, for richer, for poorer, in sickness and in health, to love and to cherish, till death us do part'.

- Wedding rings are blessed and exchanged as a sign of the vows which have just been taken. The ring symbolizes the everlasting love between the two people. (It is traditional for the bridegroom to place the ring first on the thumb of his bride, then on her second finger and then on her third, naming each person in the Trinity: in the name of God the Father, God the Son and God the Holy Spirit.)

- The priest blesses the married couple.

- Prayers are offered for the couple.

- The wedding ceremony is sometimes followed by a celebration of the Eucharist.

# Marriage is about selfless love

The following true incident speaks one truth about marriage – that it is a mirror of God's selfless love for us:

*A wheelbarrow was parked outside the doctor's clinic. In it were two very clean pillows. In a matter of minutes the doctor's door opened and out came a woman who was limping badly. She was supported by her husband who rearranged the pillows in the wheelbarrow and gently placed his wife*

# Christian beliefs about marriage

- **Married love was created by God.** It is part of God's plan for humanity and as such is sacred. In the story of the creation of the world God created Eve and then the man said: '"This at last is bone of my bones and flesh of my flesh" . . . Therefore a man leaves his father and his mother and clings to his wife, and they become one flesh' (Genesis 2.23, 24).

- **Marriage is for life.** The Church teaches that marriage is for life. First, this is to enable people to feel secure in their love. It is also important that children brought up in a family feel secure. Secondly, in marriage two people learn to love in an unselfish way and as they do this they reflect God's love. The hallmarks of a married relationship are loyalty and faithfulness.

- **Marriage is protected.** Because marriage is created by God and is part of God's plan for people it is protected in the Bible by laws: 'Thou shalt not commit adultery' (Exodus 20.14; Deuteronomy 5.18).

- **When marriages go wrong.** The Church recognizes that sometimes marriages break down past repair. In situations like these the Church supports people who are going through separation and divorce but a further marriage does not normally take place in church. Instead, people may have a civil ceremony, followed by a service of prayer and dedication. Some Christians feel hurt by this rigid standard; others feel obliged to maintain what Jesus taught (see Mark 10.2–12 but also Matthew 5.31–32, noticing how the passages differ). However, Jesus also taught people not to judge others who fail to live up to the ideal.

- **Marriage is a public announcement.** It is important to make these vows publicly – it binds a couple in front of witnesses and before God.

→ page 80

## ... more Christian beliefs about marriage

- **Marriage is the proper context for sexual intercourse.** Christians believe that the correct place for sex is within a relationship of complete commitment. In sex two people become one in a very real way – yes, physically but also emotionally and spiritually; they become completely open with each other and share their greatest intimacy. The Bible says that when two people have sex they become 'one flesh'. This is why Christians believe that the correct place for sex is within marriage.

- **Marriage is blessed by God.** God is the third partner in Christian marriage. The love which two people share in Christian marriage is a sign of God's love. When two people promise unconditional love to each other for life this shows what Christ's own sacrificial love is like.

inside. Then carefully but proudly he lifted the handles of the wheelbarrow and started to walk back home. 'That's a miracle,' said the doctor as he watched them disappear. 'That man cares enough for his sick wife to wheel her in his wheelbarrow for twenty miles. He's been here before. He will come again and again until she is better.'

(Adapted from Richard Hughes, *Taking Chances Book 2*)

We believe that God loves us for who we are. In marriage two people share God's love.

# 'Till death us do part'

Marriage is a lifelong commitment, as the following story illustrates.

*Narrator:* Katharina Jagello was the wife of Duke Wasa of Poland. Her husband was condemned to life imprisonment on the charge of treason. She asked the Swedish King Eric to be allowed to share her husband's fate.

*King Eric:* Do you realize that your husband will never be free for the rest of his life?

*Katharina:* I know that, Your Majesty.

*King Eric:* And do you realize that he will be never be treated as a duke again – he is a common traitor?

*Katharina:* Yes I know that, but whoever he is he is also my husband.

*King Eric:* But surely after all he has done you are no longer bound to him. You can leave him and marry someone else.

*Narrator:* Katharina drew her finger out of her glove to show the King her wedding ring:

*Katharina:* Read this, Your Majesty. There are two Latin words engraved on this ring: *Mors sola* – Death alone can part us.

*Narrator:* Katharina went to prison along with her husband and for 17 years shared all his hardships. It was only when King Eric died that she and her husband were freed.

(Adapted from P. Lefevre, *One Hundred Stories to Change Your Life*)

## THINKING IT THROUGH

⌛ So many people today live together instead of getting married. Why do you think they do this? What do you think are the advantages of (a) living together, (b) getting married? What does Christian teaching say about this?

⌛ What do you think about the Church's teaching about not marrying divorced people? Do you think the Church should hold to clear standards or do you think that by doing so they are lacking in compassion?

⌛ Read the following account. Do you think the Revd Peter Irwin-Clark acted in the correct way?

*The Revd Peter Irwin-Clark of St James' Church, Southampton, discovered that two members of his congregation had left their married partners to live together. He wrote them a stern letter, named them from the pulpit, and said in the parish magazine that they had 'rebelled against God' and that 1 Corinthians 5.7 specifically warns Christians to stop associating with them. St Paul is plain on the issue: you must not 'keep company with any one named a brother who is a fornicator, or covetous, or an idolater, or a reveller, or a drunkard, or an extortioner, not even to eat with such a person'. The Revd Peter Irwin-Clark says this line of action is the kindest: 'People should exercise church discipline if they love the couple and don't want them to go to Hell.'*

⌛ How do you think the Church should carry out Jesus' teaching in the following situations:
(1) A young couple who live together come to the priest asking him to baptize their baby born out of wedlock.
(2) An unmarried girl who becomes pregnant.

## BIBLE STUDY

Read Paul's advice on marriage in his letter to the Ephesians (Ephesians 5.21–33).

According to this passage:

◆ What is the proper relationship between two people in marriage?

◆ In what ways does Paul compare the marriage relationship with Christ's relationship to the Church?

◆ What do you think it means for two people to become one body?

## FOR PRAYER & REFLECTION

*Almighty God, look graciously on the world which you have made and for which your Son gave his life.*

*Bless all whom you make one flesh in marriage.*

*May their life together be a sign of your love to this broken world, so that unity may overcome estrangement, forgiveness heal guilt, and joy overcome despair.*

*Lord, in your mercy hear our prayer.*

### SOME PRAYER TOPICS . . .

❖ Ask God's help in our own personal relationships.
❖ Protection for our families.
❖ Help for people having problems in their relationships.

# CONFESSION

*Almighty God,*
*unto whom all hearts be open,*
*all desires known,*
*and from whom no secrets are hid:*
*cleanse the thoughts of our hearts*
*by the inspiration of thy Holy Spirit;*
*that we may perfectly love thee,*
*and worthily magnify thy holy name;*
*through Christ our Lord. Amen.*

At the beginning of the Eucharist we use this famous prayer, 'The Collect of Purity', to ask God to cleanse our minds so that we are properly prepared to receive communion. The word 'Collect' means prayer, and the version given here is the older one from *The Book of Common Prayer*. You may know it better in the slightly altered version used in modern language services.

## Saying sorry

- What sort of things do you have rows with your friends about?
- How do you make peace after you have had a row? Do you always wait for the other person to say sorry first or do you take the first step?

If you look at any daily newspaper you will find story after story of people who are falling out with each other: famous people getting divorced; crime rates on the increase; one country declaring war against another. It is much rarer to read stories telling of people making peace with each other.

Imagine that you are staying at a friend's house and you break one of the family's favourite plates. What would you do? How do you think your friend would react? Do you find it easy to say sorry to somebody you have wronged? What makes it difficult?

Sometimes 'sorry' is the hardest word to say, because none of us likes admitting that we have done something wrong. It is easier to 'sweep it under the carpet' and hope that nobody finds out.

As Christians we believe that when we have done something wrong (when we sin, i.e. fall short of God's design for us) we not only hurt the person we have wronged but we also hurt God because we have turned away from his perfect will for us. We therefore need to ask God to forgive us. One of the sacraments of the church is the sacrament of reconciliation, otherwise known as confession. In confession we confess what we have done wrong and ask for God's forgiveness. In return God makes peace with us (i.e. is 'reconciled' with us) and gives us a fresh start.

The priest is there at confession to help us unload the burden of our sin to God and to pronounce God's words of forgiveness.

*During the sacrament of reconciliation the priest declares Christ's forgiveness to us in a personal way.*

The sacrament of reconciliation has been called 'God's Tipp-Ex' because in it God wipes clean our slate and gives us a fresh start. Another image is to say that it is like turning a new page – we have a clean fresh page on which we can write the rest of our lives.

There is no rule about how often we need to go to confession. Within the Anglican Church there is a great variety of practice. Some Anglicans:

- make a regular appointment to see their priest-confessor. Apart from making their confession, they may also use the opportunity to talk about their spiritual life (believing that regular confession is as good for their spiritual health as going to the dentist regularly is for their teeth!);

- go to confession when they feel the need, or when something in particular is troubling them;

- do not formally go to confession but may have a spiritual director;

- ask God privately to forgive them their sins.

*The sacrament of confession is our way of saying sorry to God. It is also a time to seek spiritual direction in our lives.*

*If individuals . . . seek reconciliation and pardon in the sacrament of penance, they should be signs of reconciliation amid the conflicts of society. How could they, in all sincerity of heart, seek and find reconciliation privately in the sacrament, if in their outside lives, their work, and their business affairs they continue to exploit their fellow human beings, to pay unjust wages . . .*

(Leonardo Boff, *Sacraments of Life: Life of the Sacraments*)

# What happens in confession?

1 **Prepare before you go to confession.** Think carefully about how you have acted, thought and felt. Have a clear idea about what you are going to say. This is called an examination of conscience. Some people find it helpful to write down what they want to confess.
2 **Going in.** Some churches have 'confessionals' – a sort of box where a screen separates you from the priest. Alternatively you can arrange to make a confession informally, as a private conversation with the priest.
3 **What to say?** The way you make your confession can be informal or formal. Often you are given a set form of words on a card and say: 'Bless me, father, for I have sinned. This is . . . (how long?) since my last confession.' Then you confess your sins in your own words.
4 **The priest will talk to you.** The priest is there to help you and give guidance. He is not there to tell you off. There is probably nothing you have said which he has not heard before. It is a time to ask for help in how to overcome sin and grow spiritually. The priest will then give some advice, encouragement and a penance – this usually takes the form of a prayer or reading which the priest suggests as an act of thanksgiving for forgiveness, to be repeated in your own prayers later.

## Christian beliefs about confession

- **Confession is often called the sacrament of penance or the sacrament of reconciliation.** This describes the twofold action of this sacrament: a person says sorry to God and asks for forgiveness, and in return receives God's forgiveness and is reconciled to God again.

- **Confession gives us the opportunity to be truthful with ourselves** – it helps us to examine ourselves and come face to face with who we are.

- **In the sacrament of reconciliation God wipes our slate clean and gives us a fresh start.** God is a loving heavenly father who knows what we are really like, the good things and the bad things about us. He does not reject us because we have bad points but wants us to come back to him. 'While we were still sinners, Christ died for us' (Romans 5.8).

- **God is a loving father who actively waits to welcome back his children** who have turned away from him. This is the meaning of the parable of the Prodigal Son (Luke 15).

- **God forgives us, whatever we have done.** Some people dread confession and this fear prevents them from going. But we believe that God forgives all sins so long as they are sincerely confessed (1 John 1.9).

- **Confession is about holiness.** The aim of the Christian life is to become holy, like God. However, through sin we often fall away from God's will. God wants to re-create us in his likeness. In confession we are given a new start. God gives his power, the Holy Spirit, to help us to start again and to become a new creation. In this sacrament God comes to heal people, to re-create them in his likeness. God says: 'I love you, you are accepted, wanted and loved. Go and sin no more.'

- Because people receive God's forgiveness in the sacrament of reconciliation they should go out seeking to be reconcilers – to offer forgiveness to others.

5  **Say the act of contrition** (i.e. how sorry you are).

6  **Receive absolution.** The priest will pronounce God's forgiveness and will bless you.

# The meaning of confession

## Confession gives us a new start

The following story is told of a king of Aragon, in Spain:

*One day the king went to the jewellers with his courtiers. Whilst he was talking to the jeweller about what he wanted to purchase his courtiers inspected the other jewels in the shop. After they left the shop the jeweller came running after the king, saying that one of his most precious jewels had disappeared.*

*The king commanded that they all return to the shop. He then asked for a jug which he filled with salt. He then asked his courtiers to empty their pockets into the jug. When they had all done this the salt was poured out onto the table. In the middle of it was the diamond.*

*The king had shown generosity. He wanted to give the thief the opportunity of returning the diamond without being put to shame.*

(Adapted from P. Lefevre, *One Hundred Stories to Change Your Life*)

This is a word picture of what God does in the sacrament of reconciliation. God wants people to turn away from their wrongdoing and to start again. Like the king in the above story and the father in Jesus' parable of the Prodigal Son, God is not interested in punishing his children. He is more interested in giving them fresh starts.

## Confession is about growth

Do you have any hidden secrets which you are frightened of telling anybody about in case they think badly of you?

In his best-selling book *Why Am I Afraid to Tell You Who I Am?* John Powell explains that most people are afraid of telling other people who they really are because they might not be liked. The sacrament of confession gives us the opportunity of opening up ourselves fully to God – this takes the rawest kind of courage, but without such honesty people do not grow. God takes our secrets in his gentle hands. God looks upon us with compassion and understanding in his eyes and offers us a new start.

It is only by being reflective and getting to know our weaknesses that we come to understand them. In his book about the Seven Deadly Sins, Bishop Richard Holloway encourages people to get to know their inner secrets:

> Let us find a way of understanding . . . sin. Let us find out what sin is really looking for. Let us invite sin in for a private discussion over hot tea and ginger biscuits. (Seven to Flee, Seven to Follow)

In preparation for confession we are encouraged to spend time reflecting on ourselves and seeking out our motives. During confession we not only receive God's forgiveness but we also have the opportunity of discussing with the priest our weaknesses and strengths. It is an opportunity to understand ourselves better.

## THINKING IT THROUGH

⧗ Imagine that you are standing in front of a secret mirror. Instead of being able to reflect what you look like on the outside this mirror reflects what is happening on the inside – it shows you your secret thoughts and feelings. By yourself write down what this mirror would be telling you about yourself right now. You will need to give yourself some time to relax and really examine yourself. You may find the following headings helpful:

*Things I like about myself – thoughts and feelings.*

*Things I would like to change about myself – thoughts and feelings.*

⧗ Christians hold differing opinions about confession. Here are two:

*Opinion 1:* 'When I have done something wrong I sit down by myself and ask God to forgive me. I do not need to go to a priest for confession – it is God I need to seek forgiveness from.'

*Opinion 2:* 'I think it is important to publicly confess your sins in front of a priest. Firstly, he represents God, and it is important to hear God's forgiveness. Secondly, when we sin we not only hurt ourselves and God but we also affect other people. The priest acts as a representative for other people.'

Discuss both of these views.

## BIBLE STUDY

Read Jesus' parable about the Prodigal Son (Luke 15.11–32).

A father has two sons. The younger asks for his share of his inheritance to spend now. He leaves home and spends all the money on wild living. When he has nothing left he decides to return to his father.

- Why did the son decide to return to his father? What do you think was going through his mind?

- What had the son planned to tell his father on his return? What do you think he meant by these words (verses 18–19)?

- How did the father react when he saw his son returning home? Do you think the son expected this reception (verse 20)?

- Why do you think the father arranged for a feast to greet the son? What do you think the younger son would have felt about this? What do you think of the elder son's reaction?

This story is a good example of the process of reconciliation which is at the heart of the sacrament of confession. It is not just a matter of saying sorry – it is a whole process of rebuilding relationships which have broken. The younger son thinks about his actions (*examination of conscience*), realizes that he has wronged his father (*contrition*), goes to *confess* to his father and receives *forgiveness* and *absolution*.

## FOR PRAYER & REFLECTION

*Almighty God, our heavenly Father,*
*we have sinned against you and against our fellow men,*
*in thought and word and deed,*
*through negligence, through weakness,*
*through our own deliberate fault.*
*We are truly sorry,*
*and repent of all our sins.*
*For the sake of your Son Jesus Christ, who died for us,*
*forgive us all that is past:*
*and grant that we may serve you in newness of life*
*to the glory of your name.*
Amen.

## SOME PRAYER TOPICS . . .

- Sins against God – where you have left God out of your life.
- Sins against other people – where you have hurt them.
- Sins against yourself – where you have damaged yourself through your own attitudes and actions.
- Sins against the natural world – where you have treated animals badly or been wasteful.

# ORDINATION

## A calling

*Priests are called by God to work with the bishop and with their fellow-priests, as servants and shepherds among the people to whom they are sent. They are to proclaim the word of the Lord, to call their hearers to repentance, and in Christ's name to absolve, and to declare the forgiveness of sins. They are to baptize, and prepare the baptized for confirmation. They are to preside at the celebration of the Holy Communion. They are to lead their people in prayer and worship, to intercede for them, to bless them in the name of the Lord, and to teach and encourage by word and example. They are to minister to the sick, and prepare the dying for their death.*

Do you have a clear idea of what you want to do when you leave school (and college)? Some people feel that they have a clear idea about what they should be doing in life. Some feel that they have a calling from God to do a particular work – it may be working for a charity, or in a Third World country. It could be an everyday job – to be a mechanic, a teacher or a nurse. The word used for this calling is vocation.

Other people feel that God has called them to be part of the ordained ministry of the Church: as a deacon, priest or bishop.

In the following poem Michel Quoist describes the work of a priest.

## A Priest

*To live in the midst of the world without wishing its pleasures;*
*to be a member of each family, yet belonging to none;*
*to share all sufferings;*
*to penetrate all secrets;*
*to heal all wounds;*
*to go from men to God and offer Him their prayers;*
*to return from God to men to bring pardon and hope;*
*to have a heart of fire for charity;*
*to teach and to pardon, console and bless always,*
*My God, what a life!*
*And it is yours, O Priest of Jesus Christ!*

## Christian beliefs about ordination

● **All Christians share in the royal priesthood of Christ: we are all called to live lives of service**, praising and thanking God and interceding with God for others. However, some men and women are set apart by the Sacrament of Holy Orders to focus this calling to serve Christ and the Church in a visible way.

● **Jesus set apart certain people to preach, heal, teach, forgive sins and to exercise authority in the Church.** Jesus chose apostles for this task. As the Church spread, the leadership of the Church developed. In the second century leadership was developed by means of the threefold ministry of bishops, priests and deacons. This is still the structure of ministry in the Anglican Church today.

➜ page 88

### ... more Christian beliefs about ordination

- **The Bishop** is regarded as the direct successor of the apostles. Bishops are responsible for what goes on in their Anglican diocese. They are the focus of unity and authority. They are ordained by at least three other bishops. Although there can be only one diocesan bishop in each diocese they may be assisted by suffragan bishops. The symbols of a bishop are the mitre – the shape symbolizes the tongues of fire of the Holy Spirit which came down on the multitude at Pentecost; the staff, shaped like a shepherd's crook to show that the Bishop is the chief shepherd in the diocese; and a ring, which symbolizes that the Bishop is wedded to the diocese.

- **Priests.** The word priest comes from the Greek word for 'presbyter' (i.e. 'elder' in the New Testament). The priest looks after a parish on behalf of the Bishop, and is sometimes assisted by curates. The symbol of the priest is a long scarf called the stole, which is worn over both shoulders. The priest has three main functions in the parish: (a) to preach the Gospel; (b) to administer the sacraments – especially the Eucharist; (c) to exercise leadership – priests share with the Bishop in the office of Christ as leader and shepherd.

- **Deacons.** The Greek word *diakonos* means servant. The idea of deacons comes from the seven men of good reputation who were chosen in Acts to distribute the alms in order that the apostles could be freed for prayer and service. The symbolic mark of a deacon is the wearing of the stole diagonally over one shoulder only. The role of the deacon has come to be seen as the last step before becoming a priest. In Anglican churches people normally spend a full year after ordination as a deacon before being ordained priest. They work closely with a priest or a bishop and can, with the permission of the bishop, carry out baptisms, witness marriages, take communion to the sick, conduct funeral services, teach and preach. Today, however, some feel called to remain deacons all their lives. By doing so, they help remind the Church of the importance of this kind of ministry. Just as Jesus went among people 'in the flesh' ('incarnate' is the technical word), so deacons make the

## THINKING IT THROUGH

- ⧗ Do you feel that you have a vocation for a particular job in life?

- ⧗ Discuss with your priest when he or she felt a vocation to the priesthood – how did they hear God's call?

- ⧗ There has been much debate in recent years about whether the Anglican Church should have female priests (and therefore bishops). Why do you think there has been this debate? What do you think are the issues involved?

## FOR PRAYER & REFLECTION

*God our Father, Lord of all the world,*
*through your Son you have called us into the fellowship*
*of your universal Church;*
*hear our prayer for your faithful people*
*that in their vocation and ministry*
*each may be an instrument of your love; . . .*
*through our Lord and Saviour Jesus Christ*
*who is alive and reigns with you,*
*in the unity of the Holy Spirit,*
*one God, now and for ever.*
> *Amen.*

### SOME PRAYER TOPICS . . .

- ❖ For your parish priest.
- ❖ For your bishop.
- ❖ For people training for the priesthood.
- ❖ That each one of us may hear God's call in our lives and that we may have the willingness to listen to God, and obey.

# *BIBLE STUDY*

Read Paul's advice to the Roman Church (Romans 12.1–12).

Although this is one of the suggested biblical passages to be read during the ordination of deacons ceremony, its content applies to us all.

◆ What do you think it means to 'present your bodies as a living sacrifice, holy and acceptable to God' (verse 1). Obviously Paul is not advocating physical human sacrifice.

◆ As Christians we are not to 'be conformed to this world' (verse 2). What do you think Paul means by being conformed to this world?

◆ We are to have a right mind – a right way of thinking (verse 2). You sometimes hear people say 'I can't change, I was made this way!' Here Paul is saying that God can change the way you think and feel for the better. What qualities do you think Paul is talking about here (verse 3)?

◆ Paul compares the Christian body to a human body which has many parts but works together. He does this to suggest that we all have different gifts which we need to use for each other's good. Which gifts does he name (verses 5–8)?

◆ Do you think that you have a particular gift for ministry to people?

Church present in society and serve to remind their fellow Christians of society's most pressing needs.

● Ordination usually takes place at the diocesan cathedral.

*The person about to be ordained priest is prostrate (lying flat on the floor) as a sign of humility. The Bishop (behind the altar) is assisted by priests (left). This shows that ordination comes from the Bishop but that the person being ordained will soon become part of a wider body of priests in communion with the Bishop.*

● The ordained minister is called to serve the people he is ministering to. The importance of this aspect of the priesthood was stressed by Jesus (Matthew 20.25–28). The true follower of Christ must be the servant of others.

*A priest performs many duties, including visiting the sick and elderly – as a symbol of God's compassion and love.*

# ANOINTING THE SICK

*Are any among you sick? They should call for the elders of the church and have them pray over them, anointing them with oil in the name of the Lord. The prayer of faith will save the sick, and the Lord will raise them up; and anyone who has committed sins will be forgiven.*

(James 5.14–15)

Have you ever been really sick? What did it feel like? It can be a frightening time when you don't understand what is happening to your body. It is easy to feel alone when you are sick, especially when everyone around you is well and living life normally.

When Jesus was on earth he showed his compassion to all who were sick. He came to restore people to full health. However, he too had to suffer physically on the cross, so he understands what it feels like. In the sacrament of unction (otherwise referred to as anointing of the sick) Jesus comes close to people in their suffering and gives them the power of the Holy Spirit to help them have courage and to take away their fear.

## What happens?

- This sacrament may be requested by those who are seriously ill but also by those who seek a greater mental or spiritual wholeness.

- The priest may be accompanied by family, friends and members of the sick person's church.

- Prayers are offered for all those who are sick and the person receiving the sacrament.

- The priest lays his or her hands on the sick person in silence. This is to repeat Jesus' example when he healed people.

- The sick person is anointed with oil on the forehead and the hands as the priest prays for them.

- Everyone present says the Lord's Prayer. The Eucharist is then distributed.

- The priest says a final prayer and a blessing.

*The priest anoints the sick person with oil.*

## Christian beliefs about anointing the sick

- **A sacrament for those who are sick.** This sacrament brings God close to us in our suffering. The power of the Holy Spirit is given to help people find peace and courage and at times physical healing. This sacrament is about God's medicine, his power to heal, to bring hope out of sorrow, life out of death.

- **The sacrament is biblical.** In the letter of James the sick are told to request prayer and anointing (see the quotation at the top of the page).

One of the prayers used for blessing the sick is:

*May the Father bless you, the Son heal you*

*and the Spirit bring you strength.*

*May God keep his light in your heart,*

*may God keep you safe in his care*

*and may God stay close by you, now and for ever.*

*Amen.*

## Why does the priest lay hands on the sick?

There are a number of reasons:

- Jesus sent out his apostles to anoint the sick and heal them (Mark 6.13).

- Jesus laid his hands on people to bless them and heal them: for example, Jesus blessed children in this way, and restored sight to the blind man at Bethsaida (Mark 8.22–26).

- This practice continued in the early Church. For example, after St Paul had become blind Ananias laid his hands on him and his sight returned (Acts 9.12).

- We believe that God's Holy Spirit is released with the laying on of hands. This does not mean that it is always for physical healing. The Spirit also gives spiritual and emotional healing – Jesus referred to the Spirit as 'the Comforter'.

## THINKING IT THROUGH

- ⧗ What do we mean when we talk about different forms of sickness – physical, emotional, spiritual? Try to give examples of each.

- ⧗ How do you feel when you are sick? Share your feelings with the group.

## BIBLE STUDY

Read the advice which James gives in James 5.14–16a.

- ❖ **What does this passage say about the power of prayer? Do you think God can heal every form of illness?**

- ❖ **James clearly says that praying in faith can heal. What happens, therefore, if someone prays in faith and is not healed?**

- ❖ **What do you think of the following situation? David Watson was a priest in the Church of England until he died of cancer. He prayed for healing but died from the disease. He wrote *Fear No Evil* in the last few months of his life. In it he wrote: 'I still do not know why God allowed [my cancer], nor does it bother me. But I am beginning to hear what God is saying, and this has been enormously helpful to me. I am content to trust myself to a loving God whose control is ultimate and whose wisdom transcends my own feeble understanding.'**

## FOR PRAYER & REFLECTION

*Almighty God,*

*father of us all,*

*we pray for those who are unwell;*

*pour your blessings on them and on those who tend them,*

*encircle them with the warmth of your care,*

*strengthen them with the constancy of your love*

*and bring them peace.*

## SOME PRAYER TOPICS . . .

- ❖ For all who are sick.
- ❖ For all people who care for a sick person.
- ❖ For the bereaved – those who have lost a loved one.

# LIFE AFTER DEATH

**The Nicene Creed** contains the following statements of belief:

*He [Jesus] will come again in glory*
*to judge the living and the dead,*
*and his kingdom will have no end . . .*
*We look for the resurrection of the dead,*
*and the life of the world to come.*

## What is death?

How old were you when you first became aware of death? How did you feel?

Many of us have our first experience of death when we are young – a grandparent dies, or a friend is killed in an accident. Or a family pet dies.

In one sense death is a very ordinary experience; it is the one thing which we all do. On the other hand it is something out of the ordinary and dramatic. I remember going to my great-grandmother's funeral when I was 10 years old. As we drove through the streets on the way to the church I couldn't understand why life didn't come to a standstill. My life had. I wanted everyone to stop what they were doing – their shopping, going to the hairdresser, etc. – and be still, recognizing the very sad thing that had happened in my life: the death of someone I dearly loved.

How do you think of death: as an enemy to be resisted, or as a friend? Death need not be an enemy we have to fight. It could be a release if we were very old and tired or very ill. The knowledge and certainty of our death could even be said to concentrate our minds about how we are going to live this life.

Since Jesus was raised from the dead and promises those who follow him eternal life, Christians believe that death is not the end but the beginning of a new life with God. St Paul compared our dead bodies to seeds. When we plant them in the ground they look dead but nevertheless they grow into a new plant (1 Corinthians 15.42–44). Those close to death use similar pictures. Garvan Bryne was a twelve year old dying from a rare bone marrow disease when he explained to his parents that 'Dying is not really dying, it is just like opening an old door into a new room which is heaven . . . there you will meet the people you knew on earth and I am looking forward to that.'

*Death is nothing at all . . .*

*I have only slipped away into the next room . . . I am I, and you are you . . . whatever we were to each other, that we are still. Call me by my old familiar name, speak to me in the easy way which you always used. Put no difference into your tone . . . Laugh as we always laughed at the little jokes we enjoyed together. Play, smile, think of me, pray for me. Let my name be ever the household word that it always was . . . Life means all that it ever meant. It is the same as it ever was; there is absolutely unbroken continuity. What is this death but a negligible accident? Why should I be out of mind because I am out of sight? I am but waiting for you for an interval, somewhere very near, just around the corner. All is well.*

(Henry Scott Holland)

# The Last Judgement

Have you ever been in trouble at school and had to stand outside the headteacher's office? Or have you ever had to speak or perform in front of an audience? What does it feel like? These are examples of occasions when we are subject to judgement, which none of us likes. Christians throughout the ages have reflected on judgement because the Bible teaches that Jesus will return at the end of history to judge all people.

But what images of judgement does the Bible present? It is not primarily of someone accusing and condemning people. Rather, the New Testament portrays God as someone who actively pursues those who have done wrong with the intention of saving them and welcoming them to be with him in heaven. In the parable of the Prodigal Son, the father, who represents God, goes out of his way to help the son who has rebelled against him. He runs down the road with outstretched arms to welcome him home. In the same way, Jesus spent much of his time with tax collectors and other sinners, those whom his society judged to be outcasts.

However, in the parable of the Sheep and the Goats (Matthew 25.31–46), Jesus refers to a judgement based on how we have responded to the needs of the hungry, thirsty, those in prison, or those in need of clothing and shelter. All who have responded to such needs

have, without realizing, rendered a service to Jesus as well as the person in need, and they will be given eternal life. Those who have ignored the needs of others will not.

Christians have to hold these and other pictures in balance: God is forgiving and compassionate but nevertheless he condemns evil. As an old saying puts it, 'God hates the sin and loves the sinner.' We also need to be cautious about imagining that we can know what the life to come will be like. Jesus rebukes those (Mark 12.18–27) who ask him a question about whether a woman who had been widowed several times would have more than one husband in heaven. He tells them that heaven is not like that, with the implication that such things are beyond our present understanding.

*This is how the judgement works: the light has come into the world, but people love the darkness rather than the light. (John 3.19)*

# Hell

The Bible describes hell in a very pictorial way as a place of everlasting fire and punishment (Revelation 20.15). Many painters throughout history have represented hell in this way. These images of hell try to express the state of being far away from God, out of his loving arms. Such a state of loneliness is torture.

Hell is separation from God, the source of real joy and meaning in life. It is the final 'choosing of what is opposed to God so completely and so absolutely that the only end is total non-being' ('The Mystery of Salvation').

Some people ask, 'How can a loving God condemn people to such everlasting torture?' Christians believe that hell is not simply a punishment: it is something people choose for themselves.

*We all have a dark shadowy side. Sometimes people feel overtaken by this negative side which threatens to destroy them. Some people suffer periods of deep depression in their lives, when they feel alone, unable to engage with the outside world. It is as though they are being sucked in. Life feels like hell on earth for them.*

*We cannot believe man is free without at the same time believing in the possibility of hell . . . But God does not send people to hell.* (Richard Harries)

*There are only two kinds of people in the end: those who say to God, 'Thy will be done,' and those to whom God says, in the end, 'Thy will be done.' All that are in Hell choose it.* (C. S. Lewis, The Great Divorce)

We sometimes use the word 'hell' to describe experiences in this life which are completely opposite to God's design for us. Igor Kostin was the first photographer to fly over Chernobyl after the nuclear plant exploded. He has since returned a number of times. His trips have deeply disturbed him. The children he saw haunt him most: 'They are the ones who become innocent victims of our so-called civilization. It's hard to live among normal people now. A person who has been through hell has a different attitude. He breathes the air and feels the sunshine differently.'

---

## Christian beliefs about life after death

- **Homecall.** Christians believe that death is not the end. Instead it is a calling home to be with God. Death is a gateway through which we must pass to live eternally with God. In raising Jesus from the dead God has shown that death has been conquered. Jesus said: 'I am the resurrection and the life. Whoever believes in me will live, even though he dies; and whoever lives and believes in me will never die' (John 11.25–26).

- **The second coming of Jesus.** The Bible tells us that Jesus will return to earth at the end of time (1 Thessalonians 4.16–18). His coming will be visible and personal (Acts 1.11). His return will be seen by everyone (Matthew 24.30; Revelation 1.7). Jesus will return suddenly like a thief who comes in the night (Matthew 24.42–51). This second coming of Jesus will be a grand supernatural event, accompanied by great power and splendour (Luke 21.27–28). Death will be destroyed and Satan and all powers of evil will be overthrown and done away with for ever.

*'Hell'*
*by Hieronymus Bosch*

*. . . more Christian beliefs about life after death*

● **Signs of the end**. The Bible describes a number of signs that the end is near. Before Jesus' second coming there will be disorder – natural disasters (Luke 21.11), cosmic disorder (Luke 21.25), social disorder (2 Timothy 3.1–5; Jude 1.18), international friction: wars, revolutions, political disturbances (Mark 13.7–8; Luke 21.9–10). Before Jesus returns a number of 'false Christs' will lead people astray (Matthew 24.11–13).

● **The last judgement**. The Bible teaches that when Jesus returns he will judge the world. The final judgement will be the climax of world history (Acts 17.31). People will have to give an account of themselves (Romans 14.12) and will be judged according to their actions (2 Corinthians 5.10) – how they have served others, and in so doing how they have served Jesus (Matthew 25.31–46). Those who reject God will in turn be rejected and punished (2 Thessalonians 1.7–9). The final judgement will right the injustices of history.

● **Hell**. The Bible describes hell using the image of an everlasting fire (Revelation 20.15). The word 'hell' in the New Testament is 'Gehenna'. This referred to the valley of Hinnom outside Jerusalem, where the city's rubbish was burned. Hell stands for the state of being finally cut off from God.

● **The resurrection of the dead**. The Bible teaches that when Jesus returns Christians will be raised from the dead (1 Thessalonians 4.16) to enjoy eternal life with God. They will be given a new spiritual body which will be free from pain and sickness (1 Corinthians 15.42–44).

● **Heaven**. Before Jesus died he promised his disciples that he was going to prepare a place for them – in the many rooms of his Father's house (John 14.1–4). The Bible teaches that the earth will disappear (Revelation 21.1) and there will be a new heaven and earth (the word 'heaven' here refers to 'sky'). In heaven there is no more sickness and death (Revelation 21.4). God will dwell with his people (Revelation 21.3).

*We believe that after death we will be transformed. We can use the image of the caterpillar to explain this. A caterpillar's life is very limited; it is slow and its only interest is in eating. One day it stops eating. It spins itself a cocoon, and turns into a chrysalis. It looks dead. Then a miracle happens: out of the chrysalis a butterfly emerges into a new free life.*

# Heaven

We are not told exactly what will happen to us after death. However, the Bible teaches that when Jesus returns Christians will be raised from the dead to enjoy eternal life with God.

The Christian hope in heaven is based on what we believe about God's nature. God is immortal (God does not die) – we will have a share in his immortality. God is like a loving father who wants to give good things to his children. God is a just God who will right the evils in the world – he will judge what is wrong and reward what is right. In the Bible God has promised us life with him for ever.

> *'I am certain that nothing can separate us from his love: neither death nor life.'* (Paul in Romans 8.38)

Heaven is not like a reward for doing good deeds. A better analogy is of two people who are engaged to be married. During their engagement they look forward to a time when they can be together as man and wife. Marriage is a natural extension of their engagement – it is where their love leads them to. So also with heaven, which is where the Christian's relationship with God leads.

## The biblical picture of heaven

In the Bible heaven is described using symbolic language (harps, crowns, gold, etc.). This symbolic language is an attempt to describe the inexpressible. *Musical instruments* (harps, etc.): many people in life associate music with enjoyment. Music creates great pleasure. Heaven is a beautiful place of great pleasure.

*Crowns* suggest royalty. People go to be with God who is king of the universe. *Gold* suggests the timelessness of heaven (gold does not rust) and the preciousness of it.

Ben Travers died in 1985, when he was 95 years old. In his autobiography he said that he did not desire a tombstone but if he had to have one he would like the following words engraved on it:

> *This is where the real fun begins.*

This sentiment sums up what Christians feel about their life with God in heaven.

David Watson wrote the following as he lay dying of cancer:

> *The worst times for me were at two or three o'clock in the morning. I had told countless thousands of people that I was not afraid of death since through Christ I had already received God's gift of*

eternal life. For years I had not doubted these truths at all. But now the most fundamental questions were nagging away insistently, especially in those long hours of the night. If I was soon on my way to heaven, how real was heaven? Was it anything more than a beautiful idea? What honestly would happen when I died? How could I be sure? Indeed, how could I be certain of anything apart from cancer and death? I literally sweated out these questions . . .

I was as convinced as I possibly could be that Christ had risen from the dead, and this was the solid ground for my own future hopes. Death is not the end. There is life after death. Death is only putting out the lamp at the rise of a new dawn. (Fear No Evil)

# THINKING IT THROUGH

⧖ How does belief in life after death affect the way you live in this life?

⧖ What do you think it means to live your life by the motto *carpe diem* ('seize the day')?

⧖ Consider consciously going through one day's activities as if it were the day Jesus was returning to earth. How would you react differently? What would remain the same?

⧖ C. S. Lewis used to refer to this earthly life as 'Shadowlands' in comparison with the afterlife. Why do you think he used this word? Do you agree with this description?

⧖ How would you respond to a person who said, 'Although I believe in God and heaven I cannot believe in hell'?

## BIBLE STUDY

Read what Paul has to say about life after death in his letter to the Corinthian Church (1 Corinthians 15.20–44).

✦ Why does Paul think that our resurrection from the dead is a certainty (verse 20)?

✦ How is death described (verse 26)?

✦ To what does Paul compare the 'raising' of the human body (verses 35–38)?

✦ How does Paul describe the spiritual body after resurrection (verses 42–44)?

# FOR PRAYER & REFLECTION

Almighty God,
whose Son Jesus Christ is the resurrection
and the life of all who put their trust in him:
raise us, we pray, from the death of sin
to the life of righteousness;
that we may seek the things which are above,
where he reigns with you and the Holy Spirit,
one God, now and forever.

## SOME PRAYER TOPICS . . .

❖ Comfort for people who are hurting because a loved one has died.

❖ Ask for courage and a strong faith for those who are dying at this moment.

❖ Thank God for the great hope he has given us that death is not the end.

❖ Ask God for guidance on how best to live this life with one eye on our eternal destiny.

'Let us run with perseverance the race that is set before us' (Hebrews 12.1).

# Acknowledgements

Unless otherwise indicated on the page, quotations from the Bible are taken from the following sources: Introduction and Chapters 6, 7 and 16, from the *New International Version*, © 1973, 1978, 1984 by the International Bible Society, published by Hodder & Stoughton; Chapters 1, 3-5, 8, 9, 10 and 12, from the *Good News Bible* published by The Bible Societies/HarperCollins Publishers Ltd UK, © American Bible Society, 1966, 1971, 1976, 1992; Chapters 2, 15, 17 and 18, from *The New Revised Standard Version*, © 1989.

Prayers and extracts from liturgy are taken from the following sources: pp. 3, 14, 27, 36 (Apostles' Creed), 62, 67, 68, 71, from *Common Worship – Initiation Services*, copyright © The Central Board of Finance of the Church of England, 1997, 1998 (Church House Publishing, 1998); p. 13, from *Celebrating Common Prayer* (Mowbray, London, 1992); pp. 21, 26, 31, 39, 40, 45, 46, 58, 81, 88, 97, from *The Christian Year, Calendar, Lectionary and Collects* (Church House Publishing, 1997); pp. 32, 36, from *Canons of the Church of England* (Church House Publishing, 1993); pp. 38, 92, from *The Sunday Missal* (Collins Liturgical Publications, 1975); pp. 72, 78, proposed liturgies of the Liturgical Commission © The Central Board of Finance of the Church of England; p. 82, from *The Book of Common Prayer* of 1662, the rights of which are vested in the Crown in perpetuity within the United Kingdom; pp. 77, 86, 87 (adapted), from *The Alternative Service Book 1980*, copyright © The Central Board of Finance of the Church of England; p. 91, by John Simon.

Other quotations are from the following sources:

p. 6, James Weldon Johnson, 'The Creation', in *God's Trombones* (Penguin, USA, 1927) and Carlo Carretto, *Love is for Living* (Orbis, New York, 1985)

p. 7, James Jones, *Why Do People Suffer?* (Lion, Oxford, 1993)

p. 8, 'God be in my head': Pynson's *Horae* (1514)

pp. 10-11, Fyodor Dostoevsky, *The Brothers Karamazov*, vol. 2, trans. David Magarshack (Penguin, Harmondsworth, 1958)

p. 11, Michael Ramsey, *Introducing the Christian Faith* (SCM, London, 1961)

p. 14, 'He was born in an obscure village': David Self (ed.), *100 Readings for Assembly* (Heinemann, London, 1993)

p. 18, Robert Van de Weyer: David Self, *The Assembly Handbook*

pp. 20, 62, Charles Colson, *The Body* (Word, Milton Keynes, 1992)

p. 21, David Edwards, *What Anglicans Believe* (Mowbray, London, 1974) and C. S. Lewis, *Mere Christianity* (Fount, London, 1983)

p. 24, Maria Skobtsova: Mary Craig, *Candles in the Dark* (Spire, Hodder & Stoughton, London, 1984)

p. 27, Corrie Ten Boom, Omnibus: *Tramp for the Lord* (Hodder & Stoughton, London, 1998)

p. 29, Susan Howatch, from a lecture reprinted in *Anglican World*, Christmas 1998

p. 35, *The Book of Christian Prayer* (SPCK, London, 1995)

pp. 36, 48, Dom Antony Sutch, 'Healing society by the power of forgiveness'

p. 37, Alister McGrath, *Christian Theology – An Introduction* (Blackwell, Oxford, 1994)

p. 42, Kriss Akabusi: Ted Harrison, *Kriss Akabusi on Track* (Lion, Oxford, 1991)

p. 52, Rabbi Lionel Blue, *Bolts from the Blue* (Hodder & Stoughton, London, 1986) and C. S. Lewis, quoted in *Shadowlands* (1994), screenplay by Richard Attenborough

p. 53, C. Mercier, *Christianity for Today* (Oxford UP, Oxford, 1997)

pp. 52-3, ACTS headings: Michael Ramsey in A. Knowles, *Discovering Prayer?* (Lion, Oxford, 1993)

p. 59, Desmond Morris, *Manwatching* (Triad, London, 1982)

pp. 70, 75, 80, 84, P. Lefevre, *One Hundred Stories to Change Your Life* (St Paul Publications, Slough, 1989)

pp. 79-80, Richard Hughes, *Taking Chances Book 2* (Angel Press, East Wittering, 1985)

p. 83, Leonardo Boff, *Sacraments of Life: Life of the Sacraments* (Pastoral Press, USA, 1988)

p. 85, John Powell, *Why am I afraid to Tell You Who I Am?* (Fount, London, 1969) and Richard Holloway, *Seven to Flee, Seven to Follow* (Mowbray, London, 1986)

p. 87, Michel Quoist, *Prayers of Life* (Gill & Macmillan, Dublin, 1965)

pp. 91, 96-7, David Watson, *Fear No Evil* (Hodder & Stoughton, London, 1994)

p. 94, 'The Mystery of Salvation', report by the Church of England's doctrine commission; Richard Harries, *Being a Christian* (Mowbray, London, 1981) and C. S. Lewis, *The Great Divorce* (Fontana, London, 1971)

## Picture Credits

The publishers would like to thank the following for permission to use photographs: AKG, pp. 6, 95; Andes Press, pp. 17 (above), 21, 24, 40, 73, 83; Anglican World/J. Rosenthal, pp. 70, 89; Mark Azavedo, pp. 37, 43, 61, 62, 67, 72, 74 (all), 82, 89 (below), 90; Chris Bonnington Photo Library, p. 1; Bridgeman Art Library, pp. 15, 18, 22; British Library, p. 41; Circa Photo Library, pp. 14, 17 (below), 19; Sylvia Cordaiy, p. 28; Coventry Cathedral, p. 4; Format Photographers, pp. 11, 65 (above); S. & R. Greenhill, pp. 69, 99; Sonia Halliday, p. 32; Hutchison Photo Library, pp. 59, 64; Impact Photo Library, p. 48; National Gallery, p. 38; Carina Neibeker, p. 89 (above); Christine Osborne, pp. 5, 58; Picture Partnership, p. 39; Popperfoto, pp. 9, 12; Timothy Quallington, p. 78; Royal Signal Museum, p. 23; Sir Stanley Spencer, p. 93; Tony Stone Images, p. 27; Trip Photo Library, pp. ix, 2, 46, 51, 56, 63, 96; John Walmsley, p. 94; Janine Wiedel, pp. 65 (below), 68.

The publishers have made every effort to trace copyright holders. However, if any material has been incorrectly acknowledged, we would be pleased to correct this at the earliest opportunity.